HOW AM
THE FACE
AND TH

Take a look into the past, present, and future of Amway through the people whose personal success has contributed to the astonishing growth of the company. Along with the story of Amway and its founders, you'll read about:

- Tim Foley—former quarterback for the Miami Dolphins who found in Amway a new outlet for success . . .

- Ed and Yvonne Johnson—Texans who lost nearly everything during the mid-1980s recession, then turned themselves around through Amway . . .

- Kaoru Nakajima—a salaried man for eight years in Japan who discovered Amway and is now his own boss . . .

- Gonul Akman—a Turkish housewife whose growing Amway distributorship has triggered a wave of Amway devotees . . .

- Roomarie and Otto Steiner-Lang—who started an Amway business part-time to finance their own construction company, but found the independence they were looking for as full-time Amway representatives . . .

AND MORE!

Berkley Books by Wilbur Cross

CHOICES WITH CLOUT

Most Berkley Books are available at special quantity discounts for bulk purchases for sales promotions, premiums, fund-raising, or educational use. Special books, or book excerpts, can also be created to fit specific needs.

For details, write: Special Markets, The Berkley Publishing Group, 375 Hudson Street, New York, New York 10014.

AMWAY

The True Story
of the Company
That Transformed
the Lives
of Millions

WILBUR CROSS

BERKLEY BOOKS, NEW YORK

If you purchased this book without a cover, you should be aware that this book is stolen property. It was reported as "unsold and destroyed" to the publisher and neither the author nor the publisher has received any payment for this "stripped book."

AMWAY: THE TRUE STORY OF THE COMPANY THAT
TRANSFORMED THE LIVES OF MILLIONS

A Berkley Book / published by arrangement with
the author

PRINTING HISTORY
Berkley edition / September 1999

All rights reserved.
Copyright © 1999 by Wilbur Cross.
Book design by Tiffany Kukec.
Cover design and illustration by Robert Santora.
This book may not be reproduced in whole or in part,
by mimeograph or any other means, without permission.
For information address: The Berkley Publishing Group, a division
of Penguin Putnam Inc., 375 Hudson Street, New York, New York 10014.

The Penguin Putnam Inc. World Wide Web site address is
http://www.penguinputnam.com

ISBN: 0-425-17040-3

BERKLEY®
Berkley Books are published by The Berkley Publishing Group,
a division of Penguin Putnam Inc., 375 Hudson Street,
New York, New York 10014.
BERKLEY and the "B" design
are trademarks belonging to Penguin Putnam Inc.

PRINTED IN THE UNITED STATES OF AMERICA

10 9 8 7 6 5 4 3 2 1

Contents

Author's Viewpoint

THIS STORY OF AMWAY has been developed as a "biography" rather than a conventional history because it differs substantially from other corporate narratives in that it is an inspirational, motivational chronicle of the company in toto—its ideology, goals, beliefs, ethics, and sense of values. Unlike traditional chronological histories in which events, dates, and management documentations are the focal points, *Amway* delves deep into the soul and heart of the organization. This story presents the inner character of a company whose success depends not so much upon the corporate structure and a board of directors and the constraints of a host of shareholders, as upon the hopes and aspirations of millions of people around the globe. This is a story of faith and belief in individual achievements.

I feel well qualified, professionally, ethically, and emotionally, to present the story in an objective and meaningful manner from all rational viewpoints. I have known the Amway Corporation and many of its people for the better part of two decades. I coauthored the official history of the company, *Commitment to Excellence: The Remarkable Amway Story,* which I researched during the early years of the 1980s. (The book was published by the Benjamin Company under the editorial guidance of my good friend, the late Ted Benjamin, in 1986.) I interviewed dozens of Amway distributors over those years, and had the privilege and pleasure of spending many hours taking notes and taping discussions with the founders of Amway, Rich DeVos and Jay Van Andel. In addition, I have read just about every important book and major article by, and about, these two marketing pioneers. They inspired and stimulated me as much as any evangelists I had ever heard, with their undying faith in their beliefs and personal philosophies of ethics, goal-setting, individual achievement, and fulfillment in life's endeavors.

As a result of the inspiration and motivation derived from these discussions, interviews, and reading, I conceived the idea for a motivational, inspirational book based on their beliefs and counsel to all who would seek success in their careers and who had faith in the power of initiative. Rich and Jay gave me their blessing in this editorial venture, as well as the right to quote profusely from them and to present their outlooks and forecasts, which had been so successful in their lifetime. That book, *Choices with Clout: How to Make Things Happen by Making the Right Decisions Every Day of Your Life,* published by Berkley Books in 1995, proved to be a good seller on the market, and has since been published—or is about to be published—in eight foreign languages.

In my preface to that book, I wrote the following:

The focus is on the philosophies of relationships and living and working—the rationale and outlook that have enabled multitudes of people to achieve the goals they defined. The principles of success are not based on intellectual theories alone, but on many years of persistence, trial and error, and the resolve that they would attain the objectives they had established for themselves. While you may not agree with all of their concepts, I assure you that these principles have worked not only for Rich DeVos and Jay Van Andel, but also for their families, friends, and for millions of people around the world who have learned to live lives that are richer, more fulfilling, happier, and more rewarding in every way.

In this book you will find the same insights into the qualities of motivation and inspiration that have made Amway what it is today, and that have served as a guiding light and a resource for millions of people around the earth to create a more rewarding life.

INTRODUCTION

Multilevel Marketing

IN AN ARTICLE in the *Minneapolis Star Tribune,* in the summer of 1992, the subject of multilevel marketing, popularly known as MLM, was described as a business whose techniques ran the gamut from legitimate commercial enterprises to illegal pyramid schemes. "From Tupperware to veggie peelers, from herbs to cosmetics, from knit dresses to sexual aids," said the editorial, "direct selling is a way of life for many." As the statistics showed, at the start of the 1990s there were about six hundred direct-sales firms and MLMs in the United States, forming a $15 billion industry and involving nearly five million Americans in its sales force.

Although many MLM firms dangled exaggerated money lures, a substantial number of prospects really only wanted flexible ways to earn extra income, while others saw joining as simply a chance to buy products wholesale.

"Companies such as Amway, NuSkin, Mary Kay, Pampered Chef, Shaklee, and Sunrider International," explained the paper, "rely on meetings, one-on-one contacts, and product reputation to make themselves known and used, with no stores involved.''

As the editorial confirmed, ''The top companies stress practical training, goal-setting, self-fulfillment, recognition, enthusiasm and hard work, and the trend to an enhanced way of life. One recruiter described her people as getting 'emotionally nurtured.' Another was quoted as saying that 'working for someone else is a puppet's life.' Up-front investment is very modest, usually to buy sample kits of products, and reputable companies will buy back unsold products from distributors.''

The editorial forecast correctly that ''because MLM companies are exploring and developing ways to target narrow groups of consumers, they are likely to expand, not only in the U.S., but also abroad.''

Two years after the *Star Tribune* editorial appeared, the industry saw the publication of the book *Multilevel Marketing: The Definitive Guide to America's Top MLM Companies*. It was compiled with the help of twenty marketing experts with impressive credits. From the beginning, said a descriptive passage on the company, Amway has prided itself on the equal opportunity its business offers. ''It's an opportunity open to people from all walks of life—people with varying religious convictions, political affiliations, nationalities, ethnic backgrounds, and racial origins. Amway distributors work together to achieve financial independence by following the Amway Sales and Marketing Plan and observing the Code of Ethics and Rules of Conduct. On all other issues not specifically affecting the operation of their Amway businesses, distributors have the right to hold differing viewpoints, without jeopardizing their status in Amway or their business relationships with other distributors. Amway has been such a huge success because it is not restrictive. Because it is accessible to everyone. Because it can be tailored to meet the needs of the individual.''

In a chapter entitled ''The Time Is Right for an MLM Revolution,'' the book reported: ''We are seeing a growing number of people turning to the world of multilevel marketing, where the cost of trying something new is relatively low, but the potential rewards are high. Seeking the opportunity to increase or supplement income through openings in the growing field of network marketing often can be done in conjunction with another job. In fact, many MLM companies encourage their distributors to start out doing it part-time.''

Jeffrey Babener, a partner in a Portland law firm that specializes in MLM issues, predicted it will always be a predominantly part-time industry. He estimated that the *average* MLMer (at the start of the 1990s) should be able to make three hundred to five hundred dollars a month on a part-time basis. MLM was then actually growing at a rate of 30 percent a year, according to Babener.

Leonard Clements, an industry observer and publisher of *MarketWave,* a newsletter that focuses on the MLM industry, told *New Business Opportunities* magazine that a survey of one hundred of his readers revealed that the vast majority of them were looking to *supplement* incomes, not replace them.

''Network marketing puts the buying decision in the home, where a growing number of people would rather have it,'' said the MLM book, ''and network marketing has one significant advantage over the other avenues: It doesn't cost very much to get started and try it out. There are no franchise fees, no leases, no loans.''

''With a reputation for bringing products to the customer, MLM has been experiencing a mini-boom,'' according to a story in *Home Office Computing* magazine.

The headline on that story called network marketing and direct selling "New Age Capitalism."

The Direct Selling Association in Washington, D.C., reported at this time that 5.1 million people were now "in some form of direct selling activity," that they were dealing with "well over $12 billion in sales around the world," that nearly three hundred MLM companies were accounting for more than half of those sales, and that the number was growing "steadily."

"Markets are becoming so fragmented that it's difficult to reach them through mass advertising," said Bryan Barbieri, a marketing professor at Montreal's Concordia University. Barbieri told Canada's *Financial Post* that "word-of-mouth is one of the best ways to promote a product."

As to criticism of multilevel marketing, Barbieri countered, "If the product is a good one, then I see no essential difference from any other form of distribution. Distributors have to feel they can sell the products. If they think they'll simply make money from recruiting, then I fear they'll have trouble sleeping at night."

MLM's predictions about the "revolution" in this field of selling and marketing have proved to be right on target. According to current reports by the Direct Selling Association, sales projections at the end of the decade are almost double what DSA reported at the start of the 1990s. Other significant statistics show that there are about nine million salespersons in this field in the United States alone (not to mention the many millions in the rest of the world), that slightly more than 70 percent of sales originated in the home, that almost 80 percent of the sales dollars were the result of individuals selling on a one-to-one basis, and that 77 percent of the firms operated on a multilevel (rather than on a single-level) compensation structure.

In addition, it was clearly recorded, in surveys of the demographics of salespersons, that 99.9 percent were independent contractors rather than employees.

What role did Amway play, historically, in the creation and development of this once American, and now worldwide, marketing phenomenon?

Where does the company stand at the end of its four decades of growth and the conclusion of the twentieth century?

What does Amway anticipate for the opening years of the twenty-first century?

This book will give you some provocative insights.

CHAPTER ONE

A Global Portrait

Back in 1965, Michigan's governor, George Romney, launched "Operation Europe," aimed at increasing Michigan's business opportunities in the European market. We really hadn't considered taking Amway international, but during Operation Europe we began to realize that our person-to-person selling strategy could be applied world wide. So we jumped in with both feet by taking a few round-the-world trips to find new markets overseas. We looked for countries with a substantial middle class, with the purchasing power for our products. The countries also had to be politically stable, without high tax rates. . . . We started our overseas operation in Australia and then the United Kingdom.

Amway's international expansion provided the opportunity for Rich and me to extend the principles of American-style wealth creation into other countries worldwide. We saw Amway's blossoming into a multinational corporation as something positive for both the United States and the countries with which we did business. International trade allows each country to do what it does best and share the benefits of that specialization with consumers all over the world. Benjamin Franklin wrote, "No nation was ever ruined by trade," but some nations have been ruined by not enough of it.

Multinational firms act as ambassadors of economic freedom wherever they do business. When U.S. companies share some of the benefits of American-style capitalism with consumers in other nations, an advertisement for freedom is inevitably carried along with the goods. People under authoritarian regimes can't help but appreciate economic freedom when they see the quality of consumer goods that come from free nations. . . . So when Rich and I looked for countries in which to expand, we looked first at those countries that were most friendly to private enterprise.

—*Jay Van Andel,* An Enterprising Life, *1998*

ONE OF THE surprising facets of the Amway history and the story of the company's founding, development, and growth is that there seems to be almost no pocket of the world where the free enterprise system, or what cofounder Rich DeVos calls Compassionate Capitalism, cannot thrive. "Its growth in the countries that once made up the Soviet bloc," says DeVos, "is one proof that compassionate capitalism really works when given a chance. People want to live in a nation where they are free to try new solutions, to trade without restrictions, to compete in a free marketplace, to choose careers, and to own their own businesses. They are tired of empty shelves and broken promises. They want the things we have, things we take for granted." As he pointed out, when the Berlin Wall was breached, not only did East Germans flock across the border, but many of them jumped at the prospect when West German Amway distributors offered them a chance to start small businesses of their own and lift themselves out of poverty.

Incredibly, this pattern is repeated the world over.

Listen to Kaoru Nakajima, who became Amway's biggest distributor in Japan: "I was a salaried man working in a company for eight years. Now I am my own boss. Now I am free. Now I am selling products that make me proud. Now I am helping people in five different countries to build their own businesses. When I see so many people getting more abundant lives, I feel really excited."

Listen to Sevgi Corapci: "I was raised in Australia and was working as a podiatrist at the time I married my husband, Omit, who joined me in Australia in 1986. Omit worked in a fish market, textile industry, and later in delivery services. We were introduced to Amway in 1989 and became distributors immediately. However, we did absolutely nothing. In 1993, we were introduced to Amway a second time. Although Omit was negative at first, he later decided to become fully involved, due to a guest speaker who impressed him with the assistance provided by his sponsors. While I was expecting our second child, Omit arrived in Turkey for the entry of Amway to the Turkish market to build our business. Omit was without his wife, his child, his home, and his car when he came to Turkey, but he had made up his mind! Now we are building our business in Turkey together."

Listen to Rosmarie and Otto Steiner-Lang: "In 1980, when we started our Amway business, it was our goal to be independent business owners. In Amway, we saw a great opportunity to finance our own construction company. But we have been in the Amway business for eighteen years now, and for the last fifteen years we have operated it fulltime. We have found in Amway the independence we were looking for. This business is a doable and affordable solution for the problems in the labor market today. Amway, which represents free enterprise perfectly, postulates and promotes the initiative of the individual, reducing the burden on the public social system.''

Listen to Elisabeth and Patrick van Gelderen: ''We started our Amway business in 1981 to earn an additional eight hundred Swiss francs. But one year later, this business became our major source of income. Since 1989, we and our son have been pursuing the Amway business as a family venture, with affiliated partners in many European countries as well as in the United States and Asia. We recommend the Amway business for a successful future for other families. We are overjoyed to help other people help themselves.''

Listen to Wu Dao-liang: ''After retiring from administrative work for a reputable university in Guangzhou, I spent most of my time reading newspapers and playing mahjong—an ordinary life that an old man will go through every day. At the beginning when I started my Amway business, my family was worried that I could not handle it physically. But during these two years, they noticed I became more optimistic and more healthy. Even though I am sixty-six, I feel physically strong and young at heart. My children no longer worry that the Amway business will affect my health. Seeing my improvement, my children have followed my path and joined Amway as well.''

Listen to Xiao Feng-chun: ''I came from a very poor and remote village of Guangdong Province. I was brought up in a poor environment and my personality has always been shy, and I used to be an introvert. I studied hard and became the first one from my village admitted to a university. After graduation, I worked as a pharmacist in Guangzhou. There was no work pressure in my job. I spent most of my evenings watching TV and playing mahjong. I began to feel this kind of life was incomplete. I was then introduced to the Amway business opportunity, which I could handle without affecting my full-time job. Now I realize, on top of the fact that it does not affect my day-to-day responsibilities, I could spend my after-office hours earning extra income. Not only have I gained financially, but I am now a more open and compassionate person."

Listen to Gonul Akmun: "My daughter emigrated to Australia with her husband to improve her career as an engineer, and to explore new opportunities. They have been quite successful. However, the entry of Amway into Turkey triggered their hidden goal for building their own business in their homeland. So, they came to Turkey temporarily to start an Amway business with me. Contrary to my passive years as a housewife, I've been building our steadily growing Amway business ever since, as a full-time distributor, selling products and helping people see a new way of life for themselves. I set goals for myself as well as for the members of my group—who perceive me as their 'Aunt Gonul.' "

Listen to Barry Chi and his wife, Holly Chen: In 1992, Taiwan distributors celebrated the accomplishments of Barry Chi and Holly Chen, Amway's first Crown Ambassadors from this Western Pacific island. Holly started her Amway business in 1982, when Amway Taiwan Ltd. opened in this island nation, which is less than half the size of South Carolina. "When I was small, my family was among the poorest of the poor," recalls Holly. "As a student, I needed financial assistance to pay my school fees." Holly and Barry drove around in an old, beat-up car to recruit distributors, traversing a country where two-thirds of the terrain is mountains. "When we were down on our luck and times were difficult, we just learned to pick our-

selves up," says Holly, the mother of three grown children.
"We became better people after we overcame challenges."
Today, Holly, a former primary school teacher, and her
husband, Barry, a businessman, not only enjoy a much up-
graded lifestyle, but make regular donations to organizations in Holly's hometown to fulfill her promise to help its
citizens.

Listen to Alcimon and Marie-Chantale Colas: Alcimon
Colas sees potential wherever he looks in his beloved country. "Some people refer to Haiti as an underdeveloped
country," he comments. "But I say that Haiti will realize
its full potential in the near future." Alcimon and Marie-
Chantale have managed to escape many of the obstacles
their countrymen face, including lack of education and economic deprivation. And, yet, their former life, when he
worked as an engineer and she as an economist for the local
electric company, would have been considered enviable by
most Haitians' standards. Nevertheless, they say, people in
Haiti are no different from people anywhere else in the
world: They, too, dream of a better life. Alcimon, who
learned about the Amway opportunity from a coworker,
says, "I was very skeptical at first. I had all these hopes
and dreams for my life, and I was frustrated because I
didn't see a way of accomplishing them through my present
situation. Naturally my initial reaction was that this opportunity was just too good to be true!" But he was persuaded
to attend a follow-up meeting, where he decided to take a
chance that Amway would have the answer for their future.
That was in 1993. Since then, they have lived through the
deep troubles of Haiti's recent years, including embargos
when they were unable to obtain Amway products. But they
persevered, becoming Rubies and Pearls in 1995, Emeralds
in 1996, and then Diamonds. "Being Diamonds is a heavy
responsibility," confides Alcimon. "So many people are

watching us, depending on us.'' But, adds Marie-Chantale, ''As long as you have dreams, you have something to live for.''

Listen to Clemencia Restrepo and Luis Fernando Samper: ''Who are those crazy people who applaud and recognize the achievements of others? Who help people's businesses grow? Whom you always see smiling and happy? They are people associated with Amway. In today's world, having the opportunity to experience this unique phenomenon was what most called our attention to Amway. In the short time we have been in this business, we have experienced a change in the way we see and focus on our lives, changing our lifestyle patterns, recovering our old dreams, getting to know people, and helping people.''

Listen to Monica and Ernesto Remero: ''We are business administrators from prestigious universities in our country. However, this has not been—nor will it ever be—sufficient for finding the way to independence, as people in the traditional world know it. The old and worn-out theories are being displaced, and the real world is producing new winds of change. Amway arrived with the windmills that we needed.''

Listen to Nilufer and Merih Bolukbasi: ''We knew very well that it was impossible for us to take care of our baby while working in a demanding office environment. We thought that building our own business would give us the chance to raise our child properly, but this required a considerable amount of investment and was too risky. Then, during a family visit, we were introduced to the Amway business, and realized that this was the opportunity to build our own business with little risk, while having the time to look after our family. We appreciate working together as a family and our goal now is to build a successful business in our country and to extend it internationally."

The old-fashioned "American Dream" has gone international. These minibiographies from other countries are not isolated examples, but the real-life stories that typify a growing roster of hundreds of thousands of people who have lived their entire lives—until now—worlds apart from America or anything at all "American." Today, there are fewer and fewer places around the globe where there are no distributors of Amway products—not in the high Andes of South America, the jungle shores of Central America, the steaming tropics of the equator, the remote islands of the far Pacific, the rainforests of the Amazon, the boundless interior of China, or the snowclad reaches of the Alps.

"The export lifeblood of some countries is oil, for others it is cars, or diamonds, or food," wrote James W. Robinson in *Empire of Freedom.* However, "America's most precious export is not a commodity, natural resource, or manufactured product, but an *idea:* putting free enterprise in the hands of the common man and woman. More than one observer has noted irony in the fact that a company whose name is derived from *'American Way'* is now gaining wide acceptance in countries whose dogma for decades has been *'Yankee Go Home!'* "

Calling the history of Amway "one of America's most spectacular business success stories," Richard L. Lesher, past president of the U.S. Chamber of Commerce, stated that "Amway has had an impact all over the world in preaching free enterprise. They're the vanguard—as soon as the door opens a crack, they're in there. A lot of people in those countries go to work with Amway because it's the quickest way to change their standards of living."

On another occasion, Lesher wrote, "Should it really surprise us that when Amway opens its doors in a country recently freed from the yoke of socialism, hopeful people by the tens of thousands virtually beat down the doors to get in? Amway's winning formula of placing a low-cost business opportunity in the hands of average people, and thus giving them a means to pursue their dreams, appeals to qualities that are not simply uniquely American, but uniquely human."

In his book, *Meltdown on Main Street*, an investigation into the problems and solutions facing small businesses in America, Lesher concluded: "The small business revolution is here to stay and will have a decisive influence on our economy and our political process for years to come. Amway is in the vanguard of that revolution."

From Small Seeds to Big Orchards

One of the remarkable facts about Amway's history over the past four decades has been that many distributors who started with "basement" part-time enterprises eventually found themselves moving over the threshold into big businesses. And not a few have evolved from national to international status. Perhaps the most dramatic story is that of Peggy and Bill Britt, who joined Amway thirty years ago, after becoming dissatisfied with their jobs and lifestyle. After they had expanded the business substantially in their home territory, North Carolina, and reached out into other parts of the United States as Crown Ambassadors, they set their sights on foreign affiliations. Today, Britt Worldwide is a global empire with affiliates in more than forty countries on five continents. In the course of their developmental operations, they have spoken at rallies before as many as forty thousand people.

One of their "showcase" affiliates is Poland, which opened in November 1992 following years of political strife and Communist domination, which had long outlawed any form of free enterprise. The business in Poland has been growing strongly ever since, and within five years Amway Poland had become the third largest market in Europe— and, for the Britt team, number one. Regular functions bring the whole Britt Worldwide troupe together. By the end of the 1990's there were approximately two hundred open meetings per month in fifty cities, including Warsaw, Krakow, and Poznan, and regional seminars and rallies twice each month.

A more recent, and very significant, event was the opening of an Amway affiliate in South Africa in August 1997, with a headquarters office in Cape Town and a distribution center in Johannesburg. Although direct selling has had a long and respected history in South Africa, the Amway venture was described as ''innovative,'' since it marked one of the first times that entrepreneurial opportunities were offered to individuals. Furthermore, it was clearly stated that ''the Amway Business Opportunity is available to every South African regardless of faith, political viewpoint, or educational background.''

How did one company, born in a basement little more than a generation ago, come so far—not just in the matter of growth and prosperity, but in revolutionizing a whole concept of business and career opportunities? Let's begin at the beginning.

_____

When you look at the world
in a narrow way,
how narrow it seems!
When you look at it selfishly,
how selfish it is!
But when you look at it
in a broad, generous, friendly spirit,
what wonderful people you then find in it!

—Horace Rutledge

_____

CHAPTER TWO

The "Bootstraps" Philosophy

The year was 1959.

In terms of global time lines, it was the year that Fidel Castro ousted Cuban dictator Fulgencio Batista and assumed office as the country's premier, the year that the St. Lawrence and Great Lakes Waterway was opened to maritime traffic, and the year a University of Michigan study reported that 10 percent of American families were living on the poverty line and another 20 percent were living below it. This was also the year of business accomplishments great and small, from the introduction of the computer microchip to the first transistorized television set and the birth of the Barbie doll.

Very low on the list of newsworthy events that year was a seemingly humble happening that, though totally unpublicized and little recognized, would be the catalyst for shaping and improving the lives and lifestyles of millions of people in a way that was not dreamed of by even the participants themselves.

It was the year that Amway was born.

THROUGHOUT THE 1950s, two young entrepreneurs, Jay Van Andel and Richard DeVos, had been establishing a network of independent direct-selling distributors. These longtime friends and business partners were enjoying modest success marketing Nutrilite Food Supplements, developed by a California-based company.

Nutrilite was a multivitamin, multimineral supplement formulated from concentrate made from specially grown alfalfa, watercress, and parsley, plus yeast, minerals, and vitamins. It had been developed by Carl Rehnborg, owner of the Nutrilite company, and was a new concept in food supplements at that time. The company had a decentralized organizational structure that appealed to the two entrepreneurs. Traditionally, in most marketing firms the rewards of the employees were limited by the success of the company as a whole, and individual creativity and innovation were restricted because of the centralized nature of the organization itself. But with Nutrilite, each distributor ran his own business, benefiting by the support of the company, which handled certain centralized functions, such as research and production, and thus freed up the distributors to concentrate on making direct sales.

During the first full year, 1950, DeVos and Van Andel's sales organization grossed $82,000; this was followed by a fourfold increase the next year. By 1954, the Ja-Ri sales network (the name, pronounced ''jah-ree,'' was taken from their first names) had fanned across southern Michigan and into Ohio and Illinois.

However, Nutrilite sales started to slacken in the second half of the 1950s as increasing government regulation radically limited the claims that could be made about nutritional products. By 1958, frustration had mounted to where Nutrilite Products (manufacturer of the food supplement) and Mytinger and Castleberry (national distributor for Nutrilite) locked horns over the future of the business. Nutrilite, exploring ways to recover lost sales volume, was considering production of a cosmetics line; Mytinger and Castleberry raised fervent opposition. Nutrilite's success, they argued, depended on a dedicated salesperson whose enthusiatic presentation reflected belief in the product; that enthusiasm would dissipate if spread over several product lines.

The talks reached a flash point when the two companies launched competitive product lines. Mytinger and Castleberry began to manufacture and offer to the distributors its own brand of cosmetics; Nutrilite brought out the Edith Rehnborg cosmetics line and circumvented Mytinger and Castleberry by selling it direct to the distributors. Matters reached a deadlock when Nutrilite Products decided to sever its business ties to Mytinger and Castleberry. Aware of Ja-Ri's sales record and Van Andel's work as a mediator in the dispute, Nutrilite invited the Michigan man to come to California to head its new distribution network.

"I was flattered," admits Van Andel, "and promised to give the offer careful consideration. However, since I was not interested in working for someone else, I knew my chances of acceptance were slim."

Birth of a Venture

In one way, the offer helped to break through the business stalemate and point the way to the future. After discussing the implications, Rich DeVos and Jay Van Andel told themselves: If a company as substantial as Nutrilite was confident that one of the two partners could direct a national sales, distribution, and marketing program, then it made sense that the Ja-Ri team could do just as well on its own, and probably better.

In the early spring of 1959, Van Andel, DeVos, and seven leading distributors in the Ja-Ri sales force gathered in the little town of Charlevoix in northern Michigan. It was imperative to discuss the future of the business that they, and several thousand other distributors, depended upon for all or part of their livelihoods.

The sales plan was sound, the group agreed, but to increase sales they must seek new products. Jere Dutt, a participant at Charlevoix and later an Amway Crown Direct Distributor, recalled: "We liked the business very much, but felt it had a lot more potential."

"When you can recruit only specially skilled people," said Jay Van Andel, "you will necessarily limit the size of your sales force. The products we want must, first of all, be ones that just about anyone is familiar with and can sell. They have to meet two criteria: be of such nature that the government is not going to severely regulate what you say about them in your sales efforts; and be something that people need, and know that they need, without having to be convinced. The examples that come to mind are laundry and cleaning products."

As the Charlevoix meeting made clear, a fundamental requirement for the success of Nutrilite lay in wholehearted approval from everyone in selling. "The situation was sensitive and required careful handling," said DeVos later. "Our own distributors were divided in their loyalties: appreciative of Ja-Ri and its sponsorship, but understandably faithful to the Nutrilite product that they sold so successfully. For many of them, selling Nutrilite had become a mission, not just a means to a profit. They used the product themselves, found it beneficial, and wanted to tell the world about it."

"We couldn't expect our distributors to transfer that kind of missionary zeal to a box of laundry soap," Van

Andel recalls wryly, "but they had enough confidence in us to express a willingness to try."

"We had all the confidence in the world in Jay and Rich," said Crown Direct Distributor Bernice Hansen, one of the distributors attending the conference, "and we were willing to follow them. They had proved their worth. They had never hedged on a promise or violated a principle."

Buoyed by this new spirit of action and optimism, DeVos and Van Andel scheduled a second meeting for that spring. This time, on April 23, they met at the Hotel Leland in Detroit, along with the key distributors who had attended the first conference. The most conspicuous result was the formation of a distributor association with a board of directors comprising DeVos, Van Andel, and seven other members, all chosen by annual vote. Elected as the first president of the new association was Walter Bass, an active distributor in Ja-Ri who was considered an outstanding spokesman for his colleagues. Other notable members were Jere Dutt, Fred Hansen, Eleanor Teitsma, and Joe Victor.

With the drafting of its bylaws, the association was a reality. The fundamental question—What are we going to sell?—was now asked repeatedly. A small test was run with a unique car-wash product. Then, throughout the fall of 1959, a biodegradable liquid detergent was tested, along with other products that included furniture polish, an oven cleaner, a copper cleaner, and a laundry detergent that were manufactured by small Michigan firms. By late September, DeVos and Van Andel had established the Amway Sales Corporation and Amway Services Corporation to provide the products and services (ranging from a health plan to sales literature) to the distributors who were members of the association. The company location was listed officially as Grand Rapids, but most of the initial action took place at the homes of the founders in Ada, Michigan. "We felt

out of place in the city," recalled one of the early participants, "and far more comfortable in the friendly environment we already knew."

Coping with Growing Pains

As more and more distributors joined the organization
and the multiproduct business burgeoned, the company
passed a small but essential milestone: the hiring of its first
full-time employee. She was Kay Evans, who had been
working on a part-time basis since February 1959, handling
bookkeeping and general correspondence amid a clutter of
office furniture and file cabinets in Van Andel's basement.
This location was one of a pair of "headquarters," the
other being DeVos's basement, a few hundred feet away.

The DeVos part of the operation was administered by
another part-timer, Bob Rooker, later to be appointed Amway's Director of Shift Operations. After a day spent working for the local gas company, Rooker would descend to
the netherworld of distribution, unloading shipments and
filling orders, using the DeVos family's washing machine
and dryer as a convenient waist-level packing area. On Saturdays, he ran the mimeograph machine, stocking the
shelves with product information sheets and sales manuals
written by Van Andel.

Despite the confinement and clutter, the two makeshift
headquarters were characterized by an energetic pace and
an optimistic attitude that boded well for the future. On one
occasion, Rooker recalls, when the supply of shipping cartons was depleted, he had to pack containers of detergent
in shipping cartons hastily purchased by DeVos from a local dog-food company. Not the slightest bit fazed at the
receipt of cases marked DOG FOOD, the distributors applauded the ingenuity and persistence of their fledgling or-

ganization, as well as the popular products and prompt service emanating from Amway's offices.

Jay Van Andel and Rich DeVos worked tirelessly to provide this kind of support. It was evident in the industrious activities taking place in the basements, in their constant contacts with the growing army of distributors, and in the perpetual motion that characterized their visits to locations throughout the Midwest.

"In the beginning," recalls Kay Evans, "they were both outside men. One would be in Lansing or Detroit during the day, while the other would take off to hold a meeting at night, and they'd meet midway to discuss the business."

"Loving support" was the glue that held the business together during the day-to-day crises that commonly plague so many fledgling private enterprises. Both of the founders had married in the early 1950s, and were fortunate to have wives who were eager to share the load, especially during the increasingly demanding Nutrilite years. But now there were new family responsibilities: Nan and Stephen born to the Van Andels and Richard Jr. and Daniel to the DeVoses. Yet, even with their growing duties at home, Betty Van Andel and Helen DeVos found time to host business meetings, entertain visiting distributors and suppliers, and pitch in when extra hands were needed to fill product orders on time.

"When a group of distributors arrived at a predetermined goal," explained Helen DeVos, "we'd invite them to a special dinner and cook up a storm. And what we couldn't quite put together, we'd go out and buy. We had a great time socializing with our top achievers, and hoped that such recognition would help spur them on to their next goal."

Betty recalled the time they cooked a spaghetti dinner, although neither she nor Helen knew how to prepare it. It ended up as a gluey mass, unservable. Another time they made chili, but got their measurements wrong and made so much they were serving it to the families from the freezer for a year thereafter.

There seemed to be no end to the new members of the Amway "family" and the visitors who descended into the two basement offices. However, the available space quickly decreased as the size of the workforce increased.

"It seemed," said Kay Evans, "that more desks and shelves were being moved in every day, along with visitors. It wasn't unusual to have so many people in Jay's basement at the same time that you had to speak out whenever you wanted to change position. If you were going to move from your desk, you had to tell four or five others that you wanted out. There just wasn't any more space."

By late 1959, with space for Amway's sales and service divisions bursting at the seams, temporary relief was gained through leasing a vacant former post office in Ada and converting it into a warehouse. Six months later, Van Andel and DeVos purchased an abandoned service station down the road to house an office and some basic warehousing and shipping operations. Carole Sandy, who joined Amway in that period of fast-paced growth, recalled a momentous day in October 1960, when Rich DeVos bounded down his basement stairs and interrupted the beehive of activity. "Come on, gang," he announced, "we're moving!" Before they knew what was happening, he had pulled his station wagon up to the back door and was recruiting everyone in sight to help move desks, file cabinets, and other furnishings and equipment. Not everything went to the new quarters—just the warehouse activities from the DeVos basement went at first. Soon the small printing machine from the Van Andel basement was moved, allowing more office expansion there.

Space shortage was not the only problem that resulted from Amway's vigorous growth. Within a year of the company's birth, it was dealing with some fifteen independent suppliers, most of whom were small manufacturers who could not always deliver on time or supply the quantities required. Worse yet, they had difficulties with quality control, sometimes delivering products that fell short of Amway's strict standards, or in packaging that was inconsistent. To conduct business properly, as well as profitably, it was vital to keep products flowing in a steady stream, without interruptions caused by delayed shipments, returns, and undue warehousing.

"Amway is handling a maximum of volume on a minimum of capital," wrote Jay Van Andel in a memorandum to distributors, "so we must be cautious about tying up more capital than we can afford in any one product, while finding ourselves in short supply elsewhere."

To meet increasing consumer demand and assure reliable distribution, Amway leased six contract warehouses, strategically located in Michigan, Illinois, Indiana, and Ohio. However, Van Andel reminded their distributors, building up these reserve stocks required extra capital. The answer: "Sell more and we can stock more; increased volume increases profits, which in turn allow increased inventories."

The Do-It-Yourself Approach

As is often the case with a new business that counts on outside assistance, one supplier proved to be more consistent and reliable than the others in matters of quantity and quality alike. This was the Atco Manufacturing Company, which had diligently filled orders for one of Amway's first products, Liquid Organic Cleaner, commonly known and registered as L.O.C. By contrast, other suppliers were constantly offering DeVos and Van Andel excuses for being inconsistent in product quality or tardy in delivery.

There was one sure solution to the nagging problem: Do it yourself! After all, both founders had a long history of taking the initiative, ranging from selling and marketing to writing promotional literature, recruiting, setting up files, transporting merchandise, lugging heavy equipment, bargaining with vendors, and even making and installing signs. There were two prospective manufacturing specialists they could solicit for help: John E. Kennedy and Eugene Slaby, business partners who headed up the little Atco Manufacturing Company.

Would Kennedy and Slaby sell a half-interest in Atco and move to the converted service station in Ada, where they would operate as Amway Manufacturing Corporation? Slaby preferred not to make the move, but agreed to sell his share of the business to his partner. Thus, Kennedy became the first manager of the new in-house manufacturing operation in November 1960, a position he was to hold for eight years until retiring and selling his shares in the manufacturing division of the business.

Although the remodeled building contained floor space of only forty by sixty feet, it was further cramped by the addition of a print shop. Operating the small printing press and a mimeograph machine was young Wally Buttrick, then a high school student and one of the growing legion of parttimers who were proving that a successful business could be founded on personal initiative, dedication, and loyalty. He was a fine example, too, of the way a business built by such people rewards them with personal success and fulfillment. In Buttrick's case, after spending many long hours printing the two distributor periodicals, *Amagram* and *Newsgram*, product literature, and sales manuals, he rose through company ranks to become sales manager, and then left to devote all his time to a thriving Amway distributorship.

Looking at that first modest headquarters and cramped manufacturing site, the small group of people involved with production, sales, and services could never have conceived that their loyalty and commitment would one day help the young company to expand into a multibillion-dollar organization familiar to people throughout all corners of the globe.

The members of this dedicated group were increasingly amazed as they saw their seemingly tireless efforts, and those of the expanding distributor network, result in more sales. Not only did the orders keep flowing in, but the product lines continued to expand. Amway was now in a favorable position; it had enough flexibility and capital to experiment with new merchandise, such as water softeners, car-care products, stainless steel cookware, and at one time even a fallout shelter.

"We were always scrambling," recalls Rich DeVos, "just trying to catch up with back orders, working to train people adequately. We didn't have much time to look down the road; we were too busy meeting the demands of the day."

Business Ethics

Unlike the majority of commercial and trade organizations in America, where to associate business ethics with any kind of religious faith is about comparable to forcing employees to pray and risking the wrath of labor organizations, Amway was built on faith from the start. The founders ran the organization, as they clearly stated, "according to biblical principles of integrity, faithfulness, and truthfulness." Psychologically, this evidence of faith went a long

In Retrospect

"Imagine the scene. It's 1959 and two successful young entrepreneurs sit at the kitchen table mapping out their dreams for expanding what is already a successful effort. For several years they've been tenaciously building a direct-selling food supplement business from their homes. Then the idea comes to them: How much more could they accomplish if they widened their product selection? As good as they were at marketing vitamins and minerals, what if they were to offer household products that everyone uses every day—products such as cleaners and detergents? With what these two imaginative entrepreneurs know of multilevel marketing, they look at the lines of sponsorship and dream of them growing worldwide. Their vision sees acquaintances contacting relatives, relatives speaking with friends, and friends discussing with colleagues, as the number of people affected positively by this opportunity to achieve grows ever wider and deeper. All across America, people's hopes come alive, their personal dreams of success are realized, and a new era of prosperity spreads across borders into other lands. Supporting them are a host of high-quality products, many of which can't even be conceived of yet. One successful product becomes two, then four, and so on, as each offers distributors a new opportunity to accomplish their goals."

—*Amagram*, January 1994

way toward the success of the enterprise, for, they reasoned, the more you can build a business on trust and a *belief* in the work that lies ahead of you, the more likely you are to accomplish your goals and eventually prosper.

The same was true of ethical principles of integrity, honesty, and frankness in dealings with others, whether they were distributors, customers, suppliers, or even competitors.

A Pattern of Growth

In 1960, an historic event took place when the company moved its "warehouse" from the former post office basement into what had once been a Masonic Temple in Ada, Michigan. That year, the company's first complete year of operation as Amway, gross sales totaled $500,000, a figure that was to double during each of the next two years and make further breathtaking leaps in the years to come. This was Amway, swinging into the decade of the sixties. The company was dynamic, exciting, vibrant, and, in the eyes of the casual observer, brand-new. Yet the fact is that the roots of the company were not new at all, but had been formed and nurtured many years earlier in the persons of the two founders. History is built on history, strength on strength, durability on durability, essentials that were there from the very beginning.

In 1962, the company ventured outside the limits of the United States with the founding of Amway of Canada, its first international affiliate. The Canadian headquarters was situated in London, Ontario, in a 600-square-foot facility on Hyman Street. Two years later it moved to an office almost seven times that size. Other interesting milestones during the sixties were the recognition of the first Ruby Direct Distributors in 1962; the first Direct Distributor seminar in 1964, the purchase of the company's first airplane in 1965, the beginning of what would be a small fleet of jets; and the inauguration of the Artistry line of cosmetics, destined to spearhead company operations worldwide in the years to come. By 1968, the lines of sponsorship had spread solidly across North America and into other lands, with more than eighty thousand active distributors.

But the decade ended with a catastrophe that shook to the roots everyone employed in the Ada facilities. On a

Friday night in July 1969, the entire town resounded with what some people later described as a "supersonic boom." Immediately an increasing glow was seen in the sky, the result of an explosion in the east wing of the Amway plant. The roof of the new aerosol division collapsed into a pit of flames, fueled by petroleum derivates used in the processing of products. Newspapers the next day described "a hellish red inferno," "overwhelming fumes," and "the roar of flaring gas."

Mercifully, although seventeen people were injured, two seriously, there were no deaths or long-term hospitalizations. But the fire caused more than half a million dollars in damages, totally destroyed almost fifteen thousand square feet of plant facilities, and, of course, eventually resulted in heavy losses in product orders that could not be fulfilled.

Typical of the kind of motivational procedures the company had long since instituted, management held a meeting early the very next morning at six-thirty, to begin the urgent job of seeking new suppliers, reconstructing the critically damaged plant, and finding temporary jobs and assignments for the employees who were displaced by the explosion and fire. Steps were also taken to plan a well-equipped company fire department and establish essential courses in fire prevention and related emergency procedures to minimize physical losses and casualties in any future crisis.

The company recovered from the blow quickly and used the reconstruction opportunity wisely to make even more improvements in the plant and the area affected. Growth continued, highlighted in 1973 by the inauguration of Amway's World Headquarters Building, to be known at the time as the Center of Free Enterprise. From then on it would be the hub of Amway's global enterprises, and the site of the Ada complex of administration offices, research and development, manufacturing, and other essential facilities necessary for the efficient functioning of the heart of the company.

Unforeseen Threats in an Era of Prosperity

From time to time during its formative years, Amway had been tagged by certain critics as a "pyramid" scheme, a form of fraud in which many people are bilked when lured into placing their money in a lopsided investment in which only a few people at the top can possibly make a profit. As the Council of Better Business Bureaus described such schemes in its guidebook, *Investor Alert: How to Protect Your Money from Schemes, Scams, and Frauds*, "many pyramids attempt to establish their legitimacy by purporting to sell a product. What distinguishes these schemes from legitimate multilevel marketing businesses is that the pyramid concentrates mainly on the quick profits to be earned by recruiting others to invest, who in turn will recruit others, and so on, and on. The merchandise or service to be sold is largely ignored. The pyramid scheme, which functions much like a chain letter, then collapses as participants attempt to recover their initial, often quite large, investment by recruiting new investors from the ever-decreasing number of prospects in a given area."

Unexpectedly, in 1975, Amway's attorneys received an official complaint from the Federal Trade Commission. The FTC charged that Amway's Sales and Marketing Plan was a "scheme to pyramid distributors upon ever-increasing numbers of other distributors," that people who joined the plan were being deceived, and that there was little chance of their profiting by their association with Amway. A laundry list of other charges against the company included price-fixing, trying to control the activities of distributors by preventing them from selling Amway products through retail outlets, and exaggerating the benefits of joining the plan.

After a long and costly court battle, Amway won its case, mainly by being perfectly honest with its FTC accusers, and in effect informing them of facts that they never knew about the Sales and Marketing Plan. "We eventually came out winners," wrote Jay Van Andel in recounting his bitter experiences at the time, "but the attack convinced us of the importance of keeping the federal government apprised of who we were and what we were doing over here in Ada, Michigan."

It was quite obvious during the proceedings that the government had never before been "apprised" of Amway's real nature, business policies, ideology, and work ethics. One strong evidence of this was that witnesses, brought in to testify that they had been "misled" by the company, had never in fact put much time and effort into holding meetings or selling products. And some who had given up trying to put the Sales and Marketing Plan into effect acknowledged that the training they had received had actually benefited them in getting new positions in other fields of endeavor. The company thus convinced the court that even so-called "disgruntled" dropouts had learned so much in Amway meetings and orientation sessions that they were able to hold better jobs than in the past.

Although the FTC's case was time-consuming and needless, it was beneficial to the company in two ways: First, it cleared the air and was an excellent argument later against those detractors who, from time to time, cried "pyramid" and tried to discredit the Sales and Marketing Plan, whether for competitive reasons or personal grievances. Second, it alerted management to the fact that it needed to communicate better and more often with the government and the public at large about its marketing policies, professional integrity, and present and future plans. To that end, Anway has since opened up many more doors of communication, particularly through such technological avenues as its internet web sites and wealth of information about its global operations. (See chapter 5.)

Given its size and breadth of operations, and in contrast to many corporations its size (or smaller), the company has had surprisingly few summonses to the courts—and these largely for matters dealing with technicalities in the field of marketing and distribution. Its record is notably clear in the matter of hiring for the corporation, or recruiting for distributorships, people from minority groups, senior citizens, and those who are deaf, blind, or suffering from other disabilities. There are many Amwayites in all these categories. The first breakthrough into the ranks of Amway Diamonds by a black distributorship, for example, was achieved in 1978 by George and Ruth Halsey of North Carolina. Today there are literally hundreds of thousands of minority or disabled-person distributorships throughout the world, many of them flourishing and prosperous.

During the seventies, the company grew and prospered steadily, particularly with its international expansion into Australia, the United Kingdom, West Germany, Malaysia, Hong Kong, France, the Netherlands, and Japan.

Diversification and acquisition were often on the agenda in management conferences during this decade, as ways were sought to complement existing facilities and services with others that would be germane and supportive. As sales incentives and to provide more attractive space for distributor meetings, conventions, and rewards for goal achievements, the company purchased the *Enterprise II*, an oceangoing motor ship to serve as a conference center for those who had qualified for entrance into Diamond Club; a resort on Peter Island in the Virgin Islands for vacation-style meetings for achievers; and the Pantlind Hotel in Grand Rapids, Michigan, which was then completely renovated, enlarged, and renamed the Amway Grand Plaza Hotel, which now has a "world class" rating.

At the end of the decade, the figures showed that Amway's retail sales had escalated from a little more than $125 million in 1970 to more than $700 million. The company was really on a roll.

The year 1982 was one of economic hardship for many countries. Some businesses reluctantly pulled way back and retrenched; others had to close their doors forever. For Amway, though, 1982 was a record-breaking year. The global distributor organization numbered one million. Corporate employees worldwide numbered seven thousand. Operating from the Amway hangar at Kent County International Airport, the company's seventeen pilots and eleven support staff members kept Amway's two BAC I-11s, three Cessna Citations, and two helicopters flying a total of more than a million miles annually. Amway President Rich DeVos appeared at motivational rallies in fifteen cities across the United States. To meet this intense schedule, Amway purchased a Boeing 727 aircraft. In a move to become more active in the home electrical/electronic device field, Amway acquired the Statitrol Division of Emerson Electric Company. Corporate revenue topped $1.2 billion, and estimated retail sales exceeded $1.5 billion.

By 1984, the company's twenty-fifth anniversary, the overall product line had grown to include more than three hundred items. Over 350 million pounds of finished products were shipped from Ada. Among these products were Artistry cosmetics, produced for the first time at Ada in a new $11 million plant. According to a newspaper report at the time, "the 100,000-foot facility featured explosion-proof rooms for a high degree of safety. A lipstick casting machine was one of only four in the United States. A heat reclamation system was designed to be so energy efficient that system heat was required only during subzero temperatures. From receiving raw materials to final packaging, 175 employees could produce 95 percent of the entire Amway personal care line.''

About this time, Amway began to offer not only its own products, but the brand-name products and services of other companies through its *Personal Shoppers Catalog*, which had been founded in 1968 and which how contained items from a wide array of manufacturers, such as Kenwood, London Fog, Hamilton Beach, Seiko, Quaker, Lipton, Magnavox, Maidenform, and Playtex.

Backlash North of the Border

But the sweet was not unmixed with the sour. On a cold day in mid-November 1982, Amway's Canadian headquarters was suddenly and unexpectedly invaded by police officers, who seized records in order that Revenue Canada, the government tax authority, could place criminal charges against the company for failure to pay millions of dollars in customs duties on goods imported into Canada from the United States. Once again, Amway had to go to court, pointing out that the transfer prices for the import of merchandise had been strictly in keeping with those regarded as proper in the company's earlier agreements with Canadian customs authorities. The issues were extremely technical and complex, hinging on judicial changes—many of them unpublicized—that had been creeping into Canadian taxation and customs restrictions for years.

By the time the enervating case had dragged on for many months and right into the summer of 1983, with great drains on the time and attention of key Amway executives in both Canada and the United States, Rich and Jay decided to end what was growing into a bitter stalemate by paying substantial fines. They did so after hearing and reading repeated gloomy reports from Canadian business associations echoing a comment from the Canadian Organization of Small Business that "no matter how orderly our tax affairs may be, Revenue Canada can always find a way to destroy us."

In that mood of professional exhaustion, they also published an advertisement in the *Wall Street Journal*, which said in part, "Jay Van Andel and Rich DeVos had a very strong basis for continuing to fight against Canadian authorities. In fact, none of the lawyers ever recommended that they settle. Their decision was clearly based on the overall best interests of the individuals within the Amway Corporation. They were willing to agree to the very stiff terms unilaterally demanded by the Canadians to avoid the divisions, frictions, and tensions that would have occurred if the litigation had continued."

Everyone in Amway—most especially the distributors—were relieved that the very disruptive and distressing proceedings were now past history and they could get back to "work as usual."

The Weighty Eighties

Contrary to the gloomy headlines that began appearing in American newspapers about the economic recession taking place, Amway continued its upward—and outward—spiral. During the decade, it opened new offices in Belgium, Switzerland, Taiwan, Austria, New Zealand, Italy, Panama, Spain, Thailand, and Guatemala. Its product lines increased dramatically in consumer fields like skin care, cosmetics,

oral care, and hair care. In 1985, it launched the Amway
Water Treatment System, later described as "the most successful product launch in Amway history," with orders for
more than two hundred thousand units in the first year
alone. The company also began to offer customers lines of
educational products, like *Encyclopedia Americana* and the
Notable Black Americans series, and new telephone and
communications services from MCI.

Why was Amway, continually moving forward as it did
in that era, such a contradiction, at a time when many North
American corporations were "on hold" or critically cutting
back their operations and shaving their budgets? The answer was simple: History has shown that more people tend
to be attracted to Amway as distributors when times are
hard, jobs are scarce, prices are rising and many families
are feeling a severe economic pinch. It provides the "boot-
straps" opportunity for people to get out and do business
as an independent enterprise.

In areas of public service and the humanities, the company's leadership stressed more and more during this period—when the economy was disrupted at home and
abroad—the necessity for its employees and distributors to
be good citizens. These works extended not only into financial and social areas, but into the preservation and protection of Planet Earth. In 1989, for example, Amway
received one of its most prestigious honors ever, the
Achievement Award from the United Nations Environment
Programme for the Amway Environmental Foundation
and its extensive work in the field of ecology. (See pages
48–52.)

CHAPTER THREE

Motivation: Heartbeat of the Business

The news story was brief, located on an inside page, headed "Your Neighbors in Action," of the weekly Argus Champion, *in the small mill town of Newport, New Hampshire:*

"Aran Perkins, one of the founding members of the Disabled Veterans Club of Sullivan County, announced in his recent acceptance speech as the incoming president of the group that DVC has achieved a remarkable new goal: 85 percent of its 123 members are either employed in local firms or supporting themselves fully in self-employed businesses. 'In the latter field,' said Perkins, '18 members are making good livings as distributors for national direct-sales companies—mainly Amway. I want to introduce seven of them who are here tonight: three who have war-inflicted disabilities, two who are paraplegics, one who is blind, and one who lost two limbs in an auto accident.'

"Sarah Twombly, who has been blind since birth, talked for about ten minutes to the assembled audience at Newport High School, saying that she had joined DVC when the club

opened up~its membership in 1987, not just to veterans, but to anyone who was disabled, and had been greatly rewarded by this new relationship with others who were limited in their abilities to seek satisfactory employment. 'I held a good job in the Dorr Woolen Mill in Guild, 12 miles from my home,' she explained. 'But I found it more and more difficult to get transportation to work after my sister died, especially in the winter. Amway turned out to be the answer, and I have a growing list of loyal customers and other distributors under my leadership.'

"Readers interested in learning more about jobs for the disabled can obtain information from the Disabled Veterans Club or at the Post Office bulletin board."

IN AMWAY, MOTIVATION is the heartbeat of the business, and the ability of physically disabled distributors to function successfully—and often with far greater effectiveness than their neighbors in conventional nine-to-five jobs—is an incentive that makes a big difference.

The opportunity for those with disabilities to join Amway and become successful distributors is a little-known but very significant type of motivation. And it certainly is one that is hardly commonplace in American commerce and industry. Amway was listed in *We* magazine, a lifestyle periodical for people with disabilities, as one of the top ten companies for providing career opportunities to people with disabilities. Why is this so?

"Our list was developed using three measures," reported Dr. Charles Riley II, editor-in-chief of the magazine. "The number of self-identified disabled employees as a percentage of the company's workforce, the company's measures to successfully recruit and advance people with disabilities, and the company's general commitment to helping people with disabilities."

Better known, from the standpoint of motivation, are the programs Amway has developed over the years to reach out and communicate with people all over the world who are prospective distributors, but as yet have had little exposure to the opportunities that exist. It all started many years ago, before Amway had any business outside of North America, with what were known as "rallies."

"No aspect of the Amway world attracts more attention than its large public meetings," wrote Charles Paul Conn, a frequent chronicler of company operations, in the 1970s. "Rallies, they are usually called, or perhaps they are known by other, more colorful labels: Free Enterprise Day, Dream Night, Family Reunion, Moving-Up Seminar, Leadership Weekend, and a variety of others. By whatever name, literally hundreds of these large public gatherings are held in cities across North America on a year-round basis. Crowd size varies from a few hundred people in a hotel ballroom to upwards of 15,000 in a big-city coliseum. The speakers may be *bona fide* celebrities or merely new Direct Distributors from a nearby town. The event may draw a strictly local audience or attract people from hundreds of miles away; and the event may occupy an entire weekend or only a single two-hour session. But for all the variety among Amway rallies, virtually all share at least one characteristic: a noisy, happy enthusiasm that some newcomers find exciting, others find bewildering, but no one finds dull."

In the early days, descriptions of some of these rallies sounded more like reports on political conventions than business assemblies, as is apparent in one account from a business career magazine in 1981: "A convention atmosphere prevails as the people, wearing buttons and toting cameras, cassettes, and placards, sit in aisles and cram the doorways. The pledge of allegiance is said; preliminary speakers have had their say; and now, sensing that the magic moment is near, the convention yields to a religious fervor as the crowd bursts out with a gospel-type song, one that sets hands clapping and feet to swaying. The featured speakers enter amid flickering flashbulbs and thunderous applause.''

That description was not at all unique; it was quite familiar to those who read of Amway in the press: a tone of amusement with a touch of condescension. The rally was the most publicly visible feature of Amway's functions, the most provocative, and the one most likely to attract attention. ''There has developed, over a period of years, a public perception that Amway conventions are high-voltage events,'' wrote Conn. ''The word is out that, when Amway distributors meet, their style is somewhat more energetic than that of, say, the average downtown men's club on Tuesday noon.''

Rallies and presentations to the uninitiated are deeply rooted in Amway tradition. They go all the way back to the earliest days of the company and its growth under the leadership of Jay Van Andel and Rich DeVos. Over the years, the motivational events have become more sophisticated, and today they are high-budget, smoothly operated affairs. The biggest, most expensive, and presumably most effective attract large audiences because, in addition to education, they often include a program of entertainment by nationally known singers, musicians, and dancers. The heart of these affairs—and what most attendees want to hear—are the speeches by top, well-established distributors who relate very credible case histories about ways in which they built their businesses and climbed the ladder to success.

Keynote addresses by the founders or members of the next generation who lead the company today, which until recent years used to be in person, are now often transmitted on screen by satellite. Guest speakers are frequently featured; these are usually notables from government, religion, or the business world. Hundreds of others in dozens of countries around the globe are sponsored by individual distributorships, and it is there that the pattern of activities may more resemble the old-time rallies described above. It is not unusual, for example, for a Diamond Direct Distributor to conduct a rally of really impressive size to attract potential newcomers, as well as to provide a big pep rally for existing distributors. At these affairs the guest stars might be internationally known athletes, popular country music entertainers, television personalities, or members of Congress. Former President Gerald Ford, a close friend of the founders, has appeared frequently on the Amway scene, and former President Ronald Reagan twice appeared in rallies prior to becoming president in 1981. President Bush's first public speech following his presidency was at an Amway event in the Georgia Dome before 75,000 distributors.

As many Amway leaders have explained, the real incentive for attending rallies, conventions, or any other gathering of this kind is not the entertainment or the chance to meet notables, but the opportunity to gather information on ways to improve one's career. Attendees are, after all, independent businesspersons, not employees of a corporation, and it is in their best interest to compare notes with others in similar situations.

The Power of Motivation

If you are properly motivated, you can do almost anything you honestly believe in. Yet *belief* is just half the answer. Posted above the doorway to the football locker room at the University of Michigan one fall was a sign that was a constant reminder to players that determination can lead to excellence: *"What the mind can conceive and believe, the mind can achieve."*

That year, Michigan had an unbeaten season.

Can people really achieve anything they choose to put their minds to? Positive thinking has acquired a bad name in some quarters because a few people claim too much for it. We are sometimes asked to believe that if you think positively long enough and hard enough, you can shed pounds, acquire the skills of a professional athlete, or build a profitable and successful business. Thinking positively and believing in your abilities, however, must function within sensible bounds, Amway leaders have traditionally asserted. First, your belief must be based on facts. A politician seeking to sway opinion, for example, may think of himself as having the eloquence of Abe Lincoln, but without the insight, talents, and compassion of a true statesman, he will still sound as boring as yesterday's news.

Second, Amway has asserted all along that belief must be backed by action. And it doesn't hurt to retain a good sense of humor. Rich DeVos always liked to relate the case of the high school janitor who performed his job well, in spite of the fact that he could neither read nor write. When the school board established minimum literacy standards for all employees, the janitor was fired. Undaunted, he went on to establish his own janitorial service, which became so successful that he was soon earning more than the people who fired him. While discussing his business with his banker one day, the banker remarked, "Imagine what you could have done if you had been able to read and write."

"If I could read and write," came the reply, "I'd still be the high school janitor!"

The point here, of course, is that belief in oneself, backed by a firm commitment to achieve a chosen goal, will ultimately lead to success. Neither faith nor action alone will accomplish that. To believe in a foolish notion—even sincerely and completely—still adds up to foolishness. In a like manner, action without purpose is just wasted motion. Only when you forge unshakable faith with unbreakable will can you count on unlimited success.

The Value of Motivating Yourself

"People who attend Amway seminars and workshops," said a top distributor, "look for people who are going in the same direction that they have chosen and who are on at least the same achievement plane, and preferably a little bit higher. We advise new distributors to evaluate the standings of their friends and associates. If they are the kind who are always looking for excuses to play, rather than work, then it is very difficult for you to aim higher without exposing yourself to their ridicule or displeasure. If, on the other hand, you have selected the kinds of friends and associates who use their time productively, you are likely to do the same or risk being expelled from *their* ranks."

Arthur J. Forrest, who started his career with no money and a tenth-grade education, was once advised to accept a routine, low-paying position. He refused, managed to borrow a small sum, and went into business for himself. Years later, having founded a very successful manufacturing company, and having contributed regularly to educational institutions, he said in a speech to high school seniors, "Success is yours for the asking. A man is never a failure until he acts like one. He may be low on finances, but he is never broke as long as his process of mind produces thought that can be sold at a profit. If he desires health, happiness, and prosperity, he must claim them, for they are his birthright. He must claim them through positive thought and action."

"I Can": The Most Challenging Motivation

It is not enough, runs the Amway philosophy, to have the education, brightness, and innate capability to achieve something; you must also have the desire, and that desire must be motivated and constructive. Be wary, though, of people who claim that they are motivated and want to get ahead but who constantly are changing jobs. First they are selling products, then they are in real estate, and after that they decide they should open up a shop or get a job in an office or try their hand at some kind of craft. They never stick with any job long enough to make it a career.

Amway faces the fact that quite a few seemingly promising distributor candidates turn out to be in this category and eventually drop out. Approximately half of the people who start in Amway decide to quit at the end of their first year, when it comes time to renew their distributorships. This is not at all a high attrition rate by comparison with other multi-level and direct sales companies, and not all of these drop-outs can be categorized as confirmed "job-changers." But many simply do not have the stick-to-itiveness that characterizes the successful Amway distributor. In other words, the motivation just is not there.

By contrast, counsels the Amway philosophy, an excellent way to improve your own productivity is to be with people who know how to use time effectively. These are the individuals who say in a positive, self-assured manner, "I *can* do it!" no matter how "impossible" their objective may seem to the scoffers and their detractors. The rewards of making the right resolutions, at the right time and in the right place, can make all the difference in your life, in your lifestyle, and in your relationships with others. Once you have made choices about those relationships and then determined how to strengthen your associations in a positive way, it is vital for you to believe in yourself and your unlimited potential. If your aim is low, Rich DeVos used to say again and again, you'll hit what you shoot at: *nothing*. One of the most powerful forces in the world is the will of people who believe wholly in themselves and dare to aim high, not just once but again and again.

As Henry David Thoreau wrote, "In the long run, men hit only what they aim at. Therefore, though they should fail immediately, they should aim at something high."

DeVos emphasized again and again that *"I can!"* is the most powerful sentence you can use. For most people, that assertion works wonders. You can do what you believe you can do. The gap between what you aspire to achieve and what you actually can achieve is very narrow. But first, you must believe. The nature of your goal makes little difference. No aspects of your life are more important than the combination of faith in self and personal efforts to justify that faith. You name it—your career, business, athletics, the arts, education, church work, politics, marriage—every facet of your life can be guided by this common denominator.

You won't know what you can accomplish until you try.

This truth is so simple that people tend to overlook it. You can worry about a problem forever and never solve it—unless you try. Give things a chance to happen. No life is more tragic than that of the person who nurses a dream or ambition, always wishing but never really choosing to take the right course of action, to give the dream a chance to come true. Some people are so afraid of failure that they inevitably fail.

As the words of a popular tune had it some years ago: *"Accentuate the positive."*

The Power of Persistence

Believe not only in yourself but learn how to link your life with those qualities that can strengthen your character and enhance your lifestyle. Among the most vital of these is the power of persistence. "Based on our own experiences," Jay Van Andel used to say, "if we had to choose the one personal characteristic most associated with success it would be persistence—a strong determination and the will to endure to the end."

As he has told multitudes of distributors over the years, do not make the mistake some people do of confusing persistence with stubbornness, which exists for its own sake. Persistence has been aptly defined as "stubbornness with purpose." Distributors are counseled to support their motivation so consistently with this quality of persistence that they do not have time to listen to all the reasons why they cannot achieve their goals. "Our fondest wish for individuals bent on success," said Jay, "is not that they bring to the task a massive intellect or well-coordinated body or glib tongue or personal magnetism, but the ability and the will to persist toward their goals."

Discipline: A Strong Ally

In the Amway work ethic, motivation is also well served by the characteristics of discipline. A great Greek scholar advised his pupils some two thousand years ago: "First, say to yourself what you would be, and then do what you have to do." When motivation and goals mesh harmoniously, distributors are far more likely to achieve what they are hoping for than if they lack a definite plan of action. Goal-setting is a vital part of the process of personal motivation, necessitating discipline to keep people on track and on time.

Motivation is a dynamic tool, not some magical formula or shortcut to success. It combines the realization that you must do the things you know you should do and the realistic appraisal of those talents and skills that can be most favorably applied on your behalf. One reason why sound motivation is so effective is that success is 99 percent a matter of attitude. No matter how disciplined you are, you must be comfortable with the way you look at yourself. It is far too easy to settle for a low—or at least overly modest—opinion of yourself because that way you do not have to make any uncomfortable choices, take the extra effort, or risk failure by trying to make changes. You stay where you are, sedentary and never allowing your inner self to become a part of the person others see on the surface.

Educational Motivation

Historically, Amway has taken the stand that the successful distributor is one for whom learning—and by that is meant not necessarily traditional school learning, but keeping an open mind and continuing to pursue knowledge and experience—is a continuing lifelong pursuit. The natural inclination of people to improve their circumstances is the most powerful engine in our society and one that is attained largely through this kind of learning process. Sound judgment and the ability to meet tough challenges derive from discipline and the input of meaningful information daily.

If you can tap a pipeline to knowledge, you can be assured of linking yourself to one of the most potent and motivating forces on earth. Knowledge stimulates belief, and the power of belief is a phenomenon known to man since earliest times. If you know and believe in something with all that is within you, then you can work miracles. The following verse, from an old copy of an Amway newsletter, celebrates the role of discipline:

> *Ten times ten I tried and failed,*
> *My courage paled.*
> *Ten times ten plus one I strained,*
> *That's when I gained.*
> *Ten times ten plus two are done,*
> *And I have won.*

Motivation in the Eyes of a Professional

Shad Helmstetter, Ph.D., is a motivational expert and widely published author who has been a leading speaker to Amway organizations throughout the world. In one of his latest books, *American Victory: The Real Story of Today's Amway*, published in 1997, he provides Amway distributors with "100 Reasons Why You Should *BE* in the Business and *STAY* in the Business." One of the four major goals he discusses is "to *motivate* you to follow both your head and your heart, and make the decision to build your business."

As he says in his introduction, "I've never been one to believe in pipe dreams. If it isn't practical, if it doesn't work, I don't want any part of it. At the same time, I've long believed that most people sell themselves short. They don't get the most out of their lives. They settle for too little, and instead of their lives being exceptional, their lives are ordinary, and unremarkable, and unfulfilled."

Helmstetter, having met and interviewed hundreds of

top-level Amway distributors, has isolated six meaningful steps these highly motivated people share in common:

1. Thinking of their business as a solid, long-term business.

2. In everything they think or say, always taking their business seriously.

3. Making sure they associate with other people who take their business just as seriously as they themselves do.

4. Always thinking about, and talking about, their business as a full-time profession—not as a part-time hobby.

5. Always considering their business as being the most important career step in their life.

6. Visualizing a clear mental picture of themselves running the business and making it successful, and keeping that image always in front of themselves.

In an earlier work, *Network of Champions*, a book of self-starter ideas for Amway distributors, Helmstetter included a motivational exercise for readers to follow. He entitled it "Self-Talk for Going Diamond," or setting one's sights on this top-level distributor ranking:

I am a Diamond. I may not be there yet, but I will be, because inside of me I am a Diamond.

I have what it takes. I can go all the way to the top. I have made the choice to go Diamond.

I choose to be a Diamond. I choose to succeed in my life in every way.

I have decided to believe in myself. I'm going Diamond

and there is nothing that can stand in my way.

I have vision. I know how to dream. I see myself living that life, walking across that stage, feeling great, and knowing that I did it.

I like having freedom in my life. I like being successful in every way. I like reaching every goal I set. And I really like going Diamond.

Going Diamond is real. It works. Going Diamond is not only possible, it is something I can do.

I have set the date to go Diamond. I have the goal, the plan, and I know the date I'm going to make it.

I've decided not to wait, and not to put it off. I can do this. I'm going Diamond starting now.

I am a Diamond. I'm a Diamond in my heart, in my mind, in my plan, and in my actions.

Diamonds are people who are special. I am someone who is special. That means I can be a Diamond.

I choose to be a Diamond. In my mind, every day, I'm already there. And every day, I work hard to become the Diamond I know I am.

I know that the freedom I create is the freedom I deserve. I know that the success I choose, is the success I achieve.

This is the message I want myself to hear. I'm building my business. I'm going Diamond.

Can I do it? Yes I can! Can I be a Diamond? I already am! I'm going Diamond!

Service to Mankind

The motivations usually recognized, like those above, are ones in which individuals, families, and groups have outstanding opportunities to achieve personal career goals and develop and build profitable businesses. Often overlooked as important motivations, however, are the many

opportunities that Amway makes available for service to
the neighborhood, the nation, and indeed the world. "Amway is proud of a tradition of sharing success by contributing to the quality of life in communities worldwide," says
Steve Van Andel, chairman of the company and son of one
of the founders. Working with distributors and affiliates
around the globe, Amway sponsors programs that address
humanitarian and educational needs, protect the environment, and promote excellence and achievement in the arts
and in sport."

Amway distributors who have a deep concern for their
fellow beings and their planet are inspired and motivated
by the opportunities they have to participate in ways that
would never have been available to them in most of the
corporate world. In South America, Amway do Brasil sponsored the planting of fifty thousand trees in ten cities
throughout the country. As a result of this and its other
environmental enhancement and protection programs, Amway was presented with the U.N. Environment Programme's Achievement Award in this field, only the second
corporation to receive this prestigious honor. In Japan, the
Nature Center of Amway Japan Limited raised 310 million
yen to help environmental organizations worldwide protect
indigenous flora and fauna, coral reefs, forests, and marine
life. Other such global efforts include a Clean Up the World
project that has been especially active in Australia, Argentina, and Taiwan, beautification and conservation drives in
Germany and Austria, and an Elephant and Forest Conservation Fund in Thailand.

In other fields, the company and its distributors have
been active in such far-flung humanitarian efforts as Tele-
fono Azzuro, a well-known children's welfare rights organization in Italy; the adoption and improvement of homes
for the elderly in Malaysia; the SpielART program, dedi-

cated to supporting the arts for children in Germany; Junior
Achievement programs in the United States, Canada, and
Australia; *Biznes Start*, an educational television series in
Poland on business principles and ethics; and *Masters of
the Arctic*, an international traveling exhibition of artworks
by Polar peoples to celebrate their life in harmony with
nature.

"For those of us who are distributors and who put great
stake in volunteer work and becoming associated with helping others, our company programs and distributor sponsorships inspire us far beyond our efforts to succeed in
business alone," said an editorial in a newsletter of Amway
Canada. "In our recruiting, we tend to attract the kinds of
people we judge to be good for the business in the long
run. We take great professional pride, not only in what we
are doing, but in what we are contributing. In the United
States and Canada, for instance, our company and our distributors raised $25 million for the National Easter Seals
Society, which assists disabled children and adults. We
can't begin to tell you how much these worldwide programs
have meant to our global image."

Throughout their lives, the DeVos and Van Andel families have firmly believed that success is not measured by
how much you get, but rather, by how much you give, and
that their good fortune must be shared with others. From
their earliest days, they have donated a significant percentage of their earnings to their churches, to help those less
fortunate, or to support the community. Recent years have
seen the Grand Rapids skyline enhanced by the new Van
Andel Museum, the DeVos Women's and Children's Center in Butterworth Hospital, the Van Andel Arena, and the
Van Andel Institute, a medical research facility and a gift
to Grand Rapids and the world from the Van Andel family.
These and many more undertakings were made possible

CORPORATE MOTIVATIONS

Among the many benefits enjoyed by independent distributors, in proportion to their length of time in the business and the distributorship level they have attained, are the following:

- Invitations to major conventions, seminars, workshops, and other gatherings of company managers and distributors.
- Realty & Mortgage Services Program, making available competitive mortgage rates, the elimination of most fees normally associated with loan processing, and cash bonuses on the sale or purchase of property.
- Services of a professional move coordinator for those distributors and their families who move from one home to another or to another geographical location. Such services include not only physical help in moving, but information about schools, municipal facilities, and cost of living in the region to which they are going
- Network Savings membership cards that offer users substantial savings at hotels and motels, car rental firms, travel agencies, computer stores, service stations, eyeglass centers, and many other services.
- Drawings, for distributors who renew their businesses, offering vacations and products worth as much as $2,500.
- Expensive, and very useful, business kits, communications software, and other tools to make recruiting and record keeping easier and more reliable
- Amway GetAways package offering more than one hundred travel specials, which distributors can both use themselves and sell to their customers for a 5 percent commission.
- Amway Motoring Plan, with many on-the-road savings offers, including twenty-four-hour emergency highway service, markdowns on auto parts and supplies, allowance on auto purchases, and discounts up to 40 percent on motel accommodations.

Active distributors find many of the above, and other, benefits valuable as *direct incentives* for recruiting and retaining new distributors. The company is constantly searching for ways to implement other motivations and incentives. A recent example is the Amway Mutual Fund, which started out as a resource that would enlarge and enhance corporate retirement plans, as well as eventually reach investors outside the Amway family circle.

"It was started as a sort of paternal thing on the part of the company's owners," explained James J. Rosloniec, an Amway vice president who oversees the company's mutual fund efforts, "a kind of savings program." In the way it was set up, qualified distributors, in addition to receiving an annual cash bonus based on product sales, could also receive a profit-sharing bonus, to be paid in fund shares.

not only through contributions, but also by successful efforts to enlist community support.

This personal commitment to community carries over to the company itself. Throughout its history, and in every country in which it operates, distributors have supported innumerable projects and initiatives to help the poor, the sick, or the handicapped to build the communities in which it works, protect the environment, and promote life-enriching endeavors, such as music, theater, sports, and art.

Amway supports organizations and events such as the Public Education Fund and the Downtown Macker Jam, which help provide educational and athletic opportunities to schoolchildren in the Grand Rapids community; the Children's Miracle Network, which helps provide medical services to critically ill children in West Michigan; United Way; the Grand Rapids Symphony; and other groups and projects that help preserve and enhance the exceptional standard of living enjoyed by Grand Rapids residents.

CHAPTER FOUR

The Cutting Edge

As the world's largest manufacturer of branded vitamin and mineral supplements, Amway's Nutrilite Division continually strives to develop better natural sources. At its farms in California and Mexico, Nutrilite grows many of the plants used in its products employing the world's most advanced organic practices. Resistant plants and beneficial insects are used to control pests.

More than 125 Nutrilite scientists work full time to develop better plants, better concentrates, and new and improved products. In fiscal 1997, Nutrilite expanded its research and training efforts with the launching of the Rehnborg Center for Nutrition & Wellness in Buena Park, California.

According to Dr. David Krempin, Manager of New Science and Research, "We have scientists across the spectrum—agronomists, chemists, and biologists. Together, we help keep Amway at the leading edge of nutrition."

—Facilities brochure for R&D, 1998/99

"JAY AND RICH WERE adamant that *everything* be 100 percent," wrote Kay Evans, the first full-time employee of the company in 1959. "They made the decision without hesitation to undertake their own manufacturing and commit themselves to top quality in every way. Whether it was the way you made the product or sold it or stood behind it, everything had to be right." Although very, very few entrepreneurs would ever go out on a limb and venture into R&D, they plunged right in. Their earliest testing methods were about as practical as you could get—they used the products themselves, pushed their expectations far beyond what most customers would demand, and were their own toughest critics. Their next step, when they were satsified with a product, was to make a sample production run and toss the product into the bull ring—to the waiting distributors. If it survived the test, they went into full-scale production. If it failed, even in a trivial way, they either made the necessary improvements or took the product off the market. This historical approach to R&D, rudimentary and unsophisticated though it may seem in today's superscientific climate, was nonetheless so effective that some of those early products have endured in much their original form and continue to be heavily in demand.

The same intensity of perfection described in recollection four decades ago has not diminished. In terms of quantity, Amway today employs teams of more than 450 research and development scientists and quality assurance professionals working in fifty-seven laboratories that occupy 155,000 square feet of facilities in Ada, Michigan, alone. In terms of quality, the evaluation and analysis procedures have been established in depth, all the way down the line from research scientists to manufacturing engineers to marketing and distribution specialists who regularly inspect products and materials for their continued effectiveness and adherence to specifications under outlying market conditions.

The quality of products and of the elements that make them up is assured by both the individuals and the processes that produce them. Chemists analyze raw materials to ensure high caliber. Technicians test product formulas under simulated end-use conditions—no matter in what remote or demanding locations they may be used by customers around the world. Specialists in their respective fields focus on the details of such qualities as color, fragrance, feel, looks, and durability. Engineers are responsible for stringent testing to make certain mechanical parts—such as sprayers, controls, and measuring devices—will continue to work properly and repeatedly during the useable lifetime of each product.

The company has researched, developed, and installed state-of-the-art automated machinery of many types to test each and every bottle, carton, or other container before it is filled. And at dozens of checkpoints —from merchandise research through final assembly—products, their components, portions, and their packaging are inspected for quality assurance. In addition to maintaining constant, day-to-day quality, R&D management has adopted World Class Manufacturing Principles, the hallmark of integrity governing quality in the marketplace.

Amway exercises continuing care in the selection of sources for its materials—whether from farms, chemical plants, water wells, forests, plastics suppliers, or other derivations. When certain resources fail to measure up to its stringent standards, Amway produces its own ingredients, as in the case of nutrient-rich ingredients grown at company farms and paper fabricated at one of its own plants.

One of the toughest challenges in recent years has been to meet foreign specifications for products and components in the many countries where Amway has affiliates and sells its merchandise. Will cosmetics desired by American women be accepted in China or India? What kinds of detergents in demand in New England will also be best-sellers in Latin America or the Philippines? Are Amway vitamins, which are in such demand in Canada, going to have a steady market in South Africa? Will the line of nutritious foods and beverages popular in the Midwest find equal favor in England and Scotland? Will the compact carbon-block water treatment system so effective in many problem-water regions of the United States have any demand in Europe?

The answers to such questions as these is that Amway during the 1990s has been uniquely successful in its R&D programs to create demand for these and hundreds of other products among consumers in other countries—making them widely marketable around the globe. The success has been attributed to three different approaches:

1. Selectivity: focusing, country by country, on the products likely to have the most appeal to local consumers, and promoting them over other merchandise of lesser interest.

2. "Americanizing" the personal preferences of people abroad who are likely prospects to change their tastes and purchases when they discover U.S.-made products to be superior to those manufactured locally.

3. Actually applying R&D to adapt traditional American products for selling in certain well-defined foreign markets.

Concentration: An Amway "First" and a Boon Abroad

In addition to its reputation for quality and warranty, Amway from the beginning began to establish a reputation for innovation in product development, manufacturing, packaging, and marketing. In point of fact, its very first product, L.O.C. Multi-Purpose Cleaner, was the first biodegradable cleaner on the market, and the forerunner of other *concentrated* products that pioneered the industry trend toward concentration. As was pointed out by Doug DeVos, senior vice president—Amway Asia and Global Distributor Relations, managing director of L.O.C. "made a name for itself and for us by being concentrated and biodegradable long before it was fashionable . . . and our expert teams of scientists and researchers continue to pioneer new developments, so we can offer you the most innovative product improvements."

Product concentration has proved to be a great benefit in long-distance marketing, making it possible to effect substantial savings in weight, space, and shipping costs. This has been a boon to distribution for many foreign affiliates who may not have the advantage of the same kinds of space and transportation facilities that are found in North America.

The company can point to a long list of product innovations throughout its history, including Nutrilite, among the first multivitamin supplements on the market; a laundry compound that led the way to concentrated laundry products; a unique water treatment system; and the latest line of cosmetics and skin care products developed to meet the needs of women of many cultures and levels of society on six continents. Few people outside the cosmetic industry can appreciate the enormity of this kind of undertaking, which, not too long ago, would have been considered commercially unfeasible, if not impossible. As one regular purchaser of Amway's Artistry cosmetics commented to her distributor, "I cannot believe that the same cosmetics I prefer here in America are also the choice of women in Argentina, Egypt, Malaysia, and other parts of the world many thousands of miles from my hometown."

To its distributors, however, Amway has emphasized that the company is not always a "leader" in the introduction of a product or method of production. The field of nutrition is a good example, where the policy has been to sit back long enough to distinguish the fads from the essentials in this often controversial field. As Amway states in a brochure describing its research and development programs, "Our experts in R&D are first and foremost concerned with their responsibilities and obligations to make certain that laboratory and field tests are going to be sufficient to guarantee quality and stated results in the hands of consumers. Every item we sell under our Sales and Marketing Plan has a money-back *Customer Satisfaction Guarantee*. Over and beyond that, however, we bear total responsibility for any problems that might arise from products that are not everything we claim them to be or that might have been contaminated because of some flaw in our manufacturing, packaging, or distribution systems. Furthermore, even though Amway distributors are independent business people, they are not alone in building their businesses. Our Plan provides business principles, a Code of Ethics, Rules of Conduct, and other stipulations that we have to demand and yet make it possible for distributors to observe without jeopardy or compromise. We guarantee minimum risk to anyone who is approved to serve as a distributor, at whatever level."

Patents and Trademarks

Amway holds more than 235 patents worldwide. Though many of these are specifically in the company name, some have been issued jointly with other manufacturers who have collaborated with Amway in joint R&D programs. More than 90 percent of all Amway-branded products have been developed in-house. This is especially true in the field of branded vitamin and mineral supplements, a realm in which Amway is a world leader. In addition to the cosmetics line, these patents cover the widest range of products, including family care and grooming solutions, oral care toothpastes and rinses, shaving creams, sunscreens, weight-loss foods and beverages, cleaning solutions, water softening compounds, spray cleaners, water filters, cookware, and germicides.

Not infrequently, research scientists are called upon to *remove* something from a product to increase its benefits to the user, rather than to add new kinds of ingredients. A case in point is an innovative blend of soap, advertised with the statement "A lot's missing from our new bar soap for sensitive skin." In order to provide high cleansing power with protection for sensitive skins, Amway researchers took an existing product with an excellent market and made it totally free (100 percent) of colorants, dyes, fragrances, and preservatives. The result was the Sensitive Skin Bar, which was also allergy- and dermatology-tested, pediatrician-tested, and placed on the market as having a nondrying, natural moisterizing formula guaranteed to be nonirritating and to rinse clean.

Production Facilities

AMWAY COMPLETES NEW STATE-OF-THE-ART PERSONAL CARE MANUFACTURING FACILITY

AMWAY COMPLETES $17 MILLION EXPANSION OF PAPER PRODUCTS DIVISION

AMWAY AND RUBBERMAID JOIN R&D FORCES TO PERFECT A HIGH-QUALITY FOOD STORAGE SYSTEM

AMWAY COMPLETES $25 MILLION EXPANSION OF NUTRI-LITE LAKEVIEW CAMPUS

These are typical headlines of the late 1990s announcing Amway's ongoing and increasing operations that depend on research and development for their successful implementation. In the case of personal care products, the new plant, located in Ada, Michigan, was imperative in light of the company's increasing expansion worldwide, and the changes—sometimes substantial—in personal-care requirements from one country to another. Computer-controlled technology made it possible to meet these ever-changing needs well into the next century. They also made it possible to take environmental factors into consideration when creating the structure and design of the facilities. "As we were well aware," explained one of the designers of the facilities, "we had to locate our structures and use materials in such a way as to minimize exposure to airborne dust, dirt, and smoke. These contaminants can be devastating in the prevention of microbial adulteration that can adversely affect personal-care products in the course of preparation and manufacture."

As a result, ingredients are measured, blended in stainless steel vats, temperature treated, and packaged by computer control with all of the preciseness of pharmaceuticals. One of the most critical elements in Amway's personal care products is highly purified and pasteurized water. Using the latest technological advances in cleaning and filtration systems, Amway's water purification system combines microfiltration, via reverse osmosis, and pasteurization. First, the water is softened, it is pH balanced, and chlorine is removed. Next, the water is purified via reverse osmosis, to a level exceeding regulatory standards. This involves filtering out microsized particles by creating a pressure gradient across a semipermeable membrane. After this, the water is pasteurized at elevated temperatures before it is used for production.

All finished products are transported through sanitary stainless steel tubing to ensure hygienic standards. Much of the personal care process equipment is cleaned using the computer-controlled "clean in process" (CIP) system, of ten found in the dairy and pharmaceutical industries, which provides a safe method of cleaning that meets FDA certification standards.

The finished product remains in a closed system until the moment it is packaged on one of three state-of-the-art computer-enhanced packaging lines, including a line that shrink-wraps individual bottles, and a line for specialty custom-shaped bottles. At dozens of checkpoints, from product research and development through final packaging, Amway ensures that each personal care product meets the company's high standards for quality. Amway's commitment to quality and innovation is further demonstrated by the 450 research and development scientists and quality assurance professionals the company employs.

At a cost of $17 million, Amway's new personal care product manufacturing facility represents a significant investment to ensure that Amway-made products are of the highest quality possible. The facility was designed to produce a wide variety of personal care products, including FDA-regulated products, and incorporates the latest state-of-the-art, computer-controlled equipment and technology. An estimated thirty-five thousand engineering hours were required in the design of this world-class manufacturing facility, which was designed to meet the growth needs of the personal care product business well into the future.

Environmental factors were a key issue when creating the structure and design of the personal care facility. It was built in a location that minimizes exposure to airborne dust, dirt, and smoke, which is the single most effective step in preventing microbial contamination. Using new advances in cleaning and filtration systems, Amway's water purification system combines microfiltration and pasteurization, all in a dedicated, clean environment.

The new facilities include:

Mix warehouse. This area was designed for the efficient storage of all raw materials used to make personal care products. The inventory is automatically updated when moved using an RF (radio frequency) system.

Purified water room. All water used in personal care products passes through the purified water room. Here the water is softened, then it is pH balanced and chlorine is removed. Then the water is ready for reverse osmosis, which filters out microsized particles, and pasteurization at elevated temperatures before being used in production.

Mix room. All product ingredients are blended together in four 4,000-gallon mix tanks in this room. The tanks meet the design principles of pharmaceutical grade. Product in the tank is mixed, heated, and cooled by computer control. The mix tanks are capable of producing more than 140,000 pounds of product daily. The mix room has many special features, including regulated and filtered air flows, LTV lights at all entrances, and corrosion-resistant construction materials. The mix room's "smooth construction" ensures the cleanest possible environment. Wherever possible, utilities are recessed, encased in walls, or above ceilings to enhance the regulatory requirements for sanitary conditions. The flooring in all forty-four "wet" areas is composed of special, durable terrazzo material, less porous than other surfaces, making it easier to clean.

Packaging line. Finished products are transported through sanitary stainless steel tubing to ensure hygienic standards. The product remains in a closed system from the time it is made until bottles are filled on one of Amway's three computer-enhanced packaging lines. Packaging line #1 runs new Amway Body Series Essential products, Nature Shower Glycerine and Honey Body Shampoo, and Satinique (hair care) products. The line can run more than 200,000 bottles a day. Packaging line #2 is designed to produce Satinique products. The line's capacity exceeds 140,000 bottles a day. It also is equipped to shrink-wrap individual bottles, a requirement in some Amway markets such as Japan. Packaging line #3 is designed to run Amway Body Series, Sensitive Skin products, and travel-size products, and runs "specialty" custom-shaped bottles and packages.

Much of the personal care process equipment is cleaned using a computer-controlled system of the type often found in the dairy and pharmaceutical industries. This system provides a quick, efficient, safe method of cleaning equipment that meets FDA certification standards. The new quality assurance lab/offices area, built in conjunction with personal care, represents an investment of more than $1.5 million and offers world-class laboratories and equipment. The bright lighting in the personal care product packaging room is equivalent to hospital operating room standards, enhancing visual inspection of finished products.

Printing Facilities

The 50,000-square-foot Paper Products–West was created to meet distributor demand for products, and has enabled Amway to bring all printing operations in-house. In
addition, Amway's capacity for printing, cutting, and glu-
ing operations has been expanded by 50 percent. The project was initiated in 1991 and included facility upgrades and
an investment of over $9 million in new state-of-the-art
equipment, including a Heidelberg printing press, Bobst
die-cutting press, Arpeco color inline narrow web press,
and a Nilpeter label press.

The Heidelberg is used for all carton work, except for
Amway's Artistry skin care and shaded cosmetics, which
are produced by the Arpeco color web press. The Heidelberg runs up to fifteen thousand sheets per hour, more than
double the amount Amway's earlier equipment ran. The
Heidelberg is equipped with auto register and auto plate-
mounting features and reduces the setup time by 50 percent.
The most unique feature is a modem hookup that can be
used to troubleshoot repairs.The Bobst die-cutting press
features a ''blanking'' station that removes all carton trim,
therefore eliminating the need for manual trimming. The
Bobst is two thousand sheets per hour faster than previous
equipment and delivers cartons ready to glue.

The Arpeco color inline narrow web press can print up
to ten colors on two sides, emboss, hotstamp, and die-cut,
all inline. The Arpeco does in one line what previously took
six operations and four machines to accomplish. All cosmetics cartons are produced on this high-quality press. The
production of pressure-sensitive labels was made possible
with the addition of the Danish-made Nilpeter label press,
only the second one of its kind in the United States.

In addition to the new equipment, the Radical folder/

gluer was customized to meet Amway's unique needs to make new kinds of premium packaging. In one line it applies tear tape, handle patch, and insert to make the unique hinged-top box with locking tabs. "This expansion was the result of quality input from the staff of the Paper Products Division," said Mike King, division manager. "Self-directed work teams from the Corrugated Plant and Narrow Web Tech areas worked together to develop a strategy and recommendations for plant construction."

With the expansion, processes have been streamlined, production increased, and turnaround time for processing work has been reduced from an average of three weeks to one week.

New Premium-Quality Food Storage System

Amway and Rubbermaid Incorporated introduced in 1997 a cobranded line of premium Rubbermaid products designed and manufactured for exclusive distribution through Amway. This was a completely new line of products developed through an Amway/Rubbermaid strategic alliance. The new Amway Food Storage System by Rubbermaid is a unique combination of eloquent design and extraordinary quality, made of high-performance materials that will provide a lifetime of outstanding durability and versatility. The stackable system was designed to be used in the refrigerator, freezer, and microwave, as well as for cabinet, shelf, and countertop storage. The base containers are constructed of superior-strength polycarbonate for clarity and resistance to stains, hazing, and cracks. The containers are designed for convenient tabletop service, microwaving, food preservation, and easy identification of stored contents, with a tight seal and a design that make the products easy to open and close, as well as to grasp and clean. The food storage system was certified by the National Sanitation Foundation for its intricate design, which has no crevices to trap bacteria-harboring food residue.

Nutrilite Expansion

The expansion of the Nutrilite manufacturing facilities in Lakeville, California, in early 1998 was important enough to attract top-level dignitaries to the plant's grand opening, including former President Gerald R. Ford. "These facilities represent our commitment to the continued growth and success of the Nutrilite product line, one of Amway's most successful product lines worldwide," said Dave Van Andel, senior vice president and managing director, America and Europe, and a member of the company's Policy Board. As he pointed out, the 63,000-square-foot facility brought together operations that had been located in six separate buildings on the Lakeview campus, thus consolidating such functions as weighing, blending, processing, testing, and packaging. Today, the new building also houses a quality control laboratory, administrative facilities, a central utility plant, and a computer center.

The significance of the new, expanded facilities on a global scale can be seen in the fact that Amway Nutrilite is the largest manufacturer of branded vitamin and mineral supplements in tablet form in the world. And the global demand has been growing steadily to keep pace with Amway's increased presence in foreign lands.

CHAPTER FIVE

State-of-the-art Technical Support

Three-way calling, teleconferences, and dropshipping—the use of computerized, automated fulfillment systems—have become standard tools for today's network marketer. Fax broadcasting and voice-mail systems now let distributors deliver instructions direct to every person in their downlines. Personal computers (PCs) print out envelope labels for mailing lists with thousands of names. Do you want to go global? Wave 3 companies take care of all the customs, taxes, currency conversion, and other hassles of international business. . . . The most advanced network marketing companies today stress simplicity above all. They use computers, management systems, and cutting-edge telecommunications to make life as easy as possible for the average distributor.

—*Richard Poe,* Wave 3: The New Era in Network Marketing

AT THE TIME WHEN Richard Poe, a leading expert on business technology and communications, wrote about what he called "Wave 3" in the early 1990s, he was talking to many entrepreneurs who were just on the verge—sometimes timidly—of using computers and automation to enhance their business. At the same time, he gave recognition to Amway's management for having already been utilizing this new technology, characterizing them as pioneers who were revolutionizing the whole field of direct selling.

How far back does Amway's use of computers and automation really go? In an article published in 1979, The *Grand Rapids Press,* describing an Amway operation, "marveled at a machine that worked 24 hours a day without grumbling, executed instructions in billionths of a second, printed 2,000 lines per minute, and talked to its counterparts around the globe." The newspaper quoted an Amway employee as estimating that it would take ten thousand people to do the work of a single computer, and that without such technology maintaining close contact with the company's hundreds of thousands of distributors on a day-to-day basis would be virtually impossible.

Those statements were written at the end of the seventies, yet the computer in question was already the third generation of one that had been placed in operation to tackle Amway's complex communications and record keeping *twelve years earlier.* At the time the article appeared in the Michigan press, distributors worldwide were already familiar with such computer terminology as modems and mouses, hardware and software, programing and scrolling, disk drives and bytes—and much, much more.

In the early days of the computer, the concept of automation was so new and unfamiliar that critics actually censured Amway for, as one commentator expressed it, "taking a business that can be successful only to the degree that it relates to *people,* and *personal relationships,* and turning human beings into so many digits and figures. You just cannot sell products from a machine to a machine, and if distributors think they can, they are more than likely to end up with a lot of red ink.''

By way of contrast, an article in *Upline* had this to say to its readers, who are distributors: ''These tools and technology free you up to focus on that one most intangible part of this business, which is *relationships with people*. Your job is to develop your people and support them in building their business.''

The Direct Selling Association (DSA), by way of affirmation, has applauded the union of distributors and modern technology, even going so far as to assert that computers are the tools of independence, making it possible to ''extend and improve both customer and downline distributor networks,'' and that to resist using them is an inevitable sign of obsolescence.

Controlling the Giant

As can readily be seen, with the creation of the Internet, the World Wide Web, e-mail, and other computer-related technology, standard selling and marketing plans that have been perfected with meticulous thought and deliberation over the years could be replaced by a chaos of new—even bizarre—promotional concepts. Amway's management began keeping an eagle eye on technological developments in the computer field from the beginning, and has established very stringent policies of control.

Although anyone with access to the Internet can reach Amway websites for general information about the company, or when considering going into business as a distributor, the use of the Amway Business Network has strict technological limitations so that further access is not possible without logging in to the sites with a PIN number and password.

As the company publication *Amagram* reported in its February 1998 issue, the website was "the site where serious distributors do business," and available around the clock and around the calendar with never a pause. "Doing business with Amway is easier than ever," readers were promised, "with the additions to the ABN Amway Business Network Web site, you can now check your real time BV/PV status, transfer BV/PV to another distributor, and place orders electronically—all at no cost 24 hours a day using any Internet service provider. Join us on the Web . . . where distributors serious about their business do business!"

For any reader concerned that use of the Internet might jeopardize confidentiality, they were assured that "this site is the ideal place to conduct personal business because it offers you the utmost privacy and security." Listed as guaranteed on the ABN were the following:

- Password protection, whereby only distributors using their own private password and personal identification number (PIN) could access the site.

- Data encryption, which scrambles personal data so it is safe when passing back and forth over the Internet between the distributor and Amway.

- Personalized transactions, so that only the distributor in question, using a secret password, could order products, check volume, or transfer bonuses.

- Continued expansion, so that more and more personal business information and transactions will be able to be downloaded and processed in the future.

This site has been enhanced so that it now provides other Amway business bulletins, hot-breaking news about the industry, stories about new foreign affiliates, preview copies of *Amagram* and *Newsgram* before they are shipped in the mail, and price-list updates for software users. Looking at the overall picture, it is easy to see that access to Amway websites is a strong selling point for attracting new distributors to the business. And the goal is to improve the ABN continually to enhance communication and to provide a ready and very useful medium of instant feedback from distributors in the field, no matter how far away they may be located.

The Creation of a New Web Concept: *e-business*

- CD-ROMS

- Electronic ordering from PCs

- Personal home pages

- An exclusive distributor-only website with business data

- Public websites with product, opportunity, and corporate information

These examples of a new electronic advantage called *e-business* were developed in 1999 to keep abreast of constantly changing business operational improvements, new ways of doing business, global growth potential, and what the company refers to as the "tradition of innovation."

"Just look at this *e-business* menu," wrote Dave Van Andel, senior vice president, Americas and Europe, to worldwide distributors. "The bottom line? By having more efficient *e-business* tools, you can leverage to an even greater degree what's made Amway famous: person-to-person marketing. All in all, it's Amway's unbeatable combination of high-tech and high-touch. And that can mean only one thing for all of us: high growth!''

The menu he listed:

Amway Instant Order, making it possible to order electronically with a personal computer, twenty-four hours a day, seven days a week. Instant Order automatically enters prices, sales tax, PV/BV, distributor cost and suggested retail, and provides immediate verification of product availability.

Products & Services CD-ROM, to access this complete multimedia resource for product information, video previewing, price checks, and ordering through Instant Order.

Amway Automated Order Center, creating capabilities for using Touch-Tone phones to order all day, every day. With the distributor's authorization, AAOC also accepts catalog orders from customers.

Personal Home Page, making it possible for distributors to create their own personal home page on the Internet for less than it costs to print business cards, and tell the world about their Amway business.

Amway Public Websites, providing facts about Amway's history, products, opportunities, and community involvement on the company's public website, *www.amway.com,* with links to the Amway U.S. and Canadian websites.

ABN Amway Business Network, a website exclusively for independent distributors at *www.amway-abn.com,* to provide personal and group PV/BV totals, tax information, current price files, software updates, electronic versions of Amway publications, and answers to user's questions.

"In addition to all the above," assured Van Andel, "Amway will continue to expand its *e-business* activity to ensure that this opportunity remains at the leading edge for today's—and tomorrow's—entrepreneurs."

Other Computer-Related Advances

In the mid-1990s, Amway created and market-tested its first catalogs to be produced on CD-ROM (Compact Disk Read-Only Memory), to complement the lists of products and services that had traditionally been published only in print. What this innovation meant was that distributors could now place a water-thin, four-and-a-half-inch disk in their computers and order, electronically, more than a thousand products and/or services. Because of multimedia components, these CD-ROM incorporate video and sound, as well as illustrations, graphics, and text.

In the matter of training and orientation, it is evident that history is being made every day as Amway uses these fields of technology in regions thousands of miles away from company headquarters. As one computer expert expressed it, "We have shrivelled the globe and brought all humanity together in a way historians could not have conceived of in the past." Even the language barriers are being melted as newer types of computers are being programed to translate instructions and information into more than eighty languages—and almost instantaneously.

Website for a New Career

Also in the mid-1990s, the company began a program of using its websites to inform prospects about the advantages and rewards of becoming a direct distributor in Amway. Computer users who downloaded one such website, for example, were provided with the following introductory information in a program entitled "Business Opportunity."

The Amway Opportunity offers distributors many benefits. Some are financial, others are intangibles, such as peer recognition, pride in achievement, the joy of helping others, working with family, and the esteem of owning your own business.

Let's begin with **Income Potential**

As an Amway distributor, you can earn income many different ways. For instance, in the U.S. and Canada, you can earn income in at least ten different ways. They include retail profit (the difference between Distributor Cost and the Retail Price) and nine different bonuses rewarding various levels of accomplishment.

Now let's go to **Special Leadership Programs**

As you qualify at various levels of achievement, you may be eligible to attend various Amway leadership programs:

Annual Business Meetings: *In countries around the world, company-paid invitations are extended to Amway leaders to meet in a business-building atmosphere.*

Variety of Special Programs: When your business qualifies at a specific distributor level, a special invitation occurs. Imagine your special day at an Amway facility, your own success story featured in our distributor magazine, and your name and picture added to the Distributor Hall of Fame in Amway's World Headquarters.

Go to **Low Start-up Costs**

With an Amway Business Kit being the only start-up cost, virtually anyone can own an Amway business. Compared with other business opportunities, initial costs for starting an Amway business are intentionally low, priced affordably for nearly anyone with a desire to invest in their future.

Go to **Low Risk**

Our product-buy-back policy and no inventory requirement ensure a very low risk when starting an Amway business. Our Satisfaction Guarantee *has always been a measure of confidence in the quality and value of Amway products, one more way Amway supports the business opportunity for distributors.*

Go to **Performance Based**

Amway is a performance-based business that rewards people in direct proportion to their effort. The bigger the financial goal the more time and effort a distributor will need to put into his or her business. With an Amway business, a distributor can work as much or as little as he or she likes. The rewards are based directly on the distributor's accomplishments.

Go to **Direct Selling Is the Trend**

Twenty-five million people worldwide are engaged in direct selling, an $80 billion industry. As people become busier, they're looking for ways to save time on routine tasks, such as shopping for everyday needs. Direct selling fills this need nicely because Amway distributors deliver products to their doors. In addition, Amway is one of the oldest and largest direct selling companies in the world.

Go to **Flexibility**

Goals and rewards are different for each distributor. You have the flexibility of working part time while keeping a full-time job or building an Amway business into a full-time career. You choose the time you invest in building your Amway business.

Go to **Product Support**

The Amway business opportunity is supported by a diverse line of hundreds of quality Amway products and, in many markets, thousands of other brand-name products and services. Amway has established a reputation for innovation in developing top quality products and packaging.

Go to **Corporate Support**

More than 14,000 people worldwide are employed in Amway manufacturing, administration, and distribution facilities totaling 10 million square feet (929,000 square meters). Amway manufactures products in the United States, China, and Korea and maintains product warehousing facilities around the globe.

*Go to **Equality of Opportunity***

Anyone starting an Amway business gets in at the same level. Each new distributor has the same opportunity to surpass the most successful distributor, and the business opportunity is continually improved. The Amway opportunity has been imitated often, but the level of support Amway provides its distributors is difficult to duplicate.

For those users of the Internet who then want further information about Amway, its history and background, its worldwide locations, its management, its distributors, or recent news releases that pinpoint events in the company's operations during the past year, there are other websites that will open the information doors. (See the end of this chapter for examples from some of Amway's active websites.) You can also *ask* questions by going to Anway's Information Center home page at **www.amway.com/InfoCenter/**. In anticipation of this, and with the focus on some key questions that are often asked, Amway has prepared a Q&A page with a dozen or so entries.

Six questions from this website follow, as examples of FAQs (a popular Internet term meaning "Frequently Asked Questions").

Why is there so much criticism of Amway on the Internet?
The Internet has provided a forum for millions to express their personal experiences and opinions, and some users have chosen to post information critical of Amway in public areas of the Internet. This information must be considered within the context of more than 3 million people worldwide who saw enough benefit in their Amway businesses to renew their distributorships for another year. Amway supports individuals' First Amendment rights to free speech

and recognizes the Internet as a valuable communications tool. In exercising their First Amendment rights, however, individuals must accept the responsibility of ensuring the information they publish is accurate, fair and true. There's hardly a reputable, respected corporation left that hasn't been the target of a Website. Amway is only one of a growing number of companies and organizations that are calling for the responsible use of the Internet. While critics are entitled to their views, the fact remains that the viability and legitimacy of the Amway opportunity has been tested and proven through nearly 40 years of phenomenal success as a low-cost, low-risk opportunity open to all.

Is it true that Amway endorses one religion?

No, the Amway business is open to anyone, regardless of religious, political or other personal beliefs; gender; or race. Although we don't keep records on this, we believe you would find a great diversity of religious faiths, including Judaism, Islam, Hinduism, Buddhism, Christianity, etc., among our distributors and employees. The U.S. Amway Distributor Association Board has formulated speakers' guidelines about the use of a business meeting to pitch individual beliefs about religion or politics. Moreover, Amway offers opportunity to any ethnic group, young and old, women and men, educated or not, disabled or not. The success of our distributors in 49 affiliate markets around the globe shows that our business opportunity transcends borders and differences in language, culture, politics, and personal beliefs.

Why is there such a perceived focus in the Amway business on material things?

This is a business, and a main reason people work at any business is to earn money that not only will help them pay

*their bills, but also meet other goals. Those may be short-
or long-term goals, and they could be large (like buying a
new house) or small (like saving for a vacation). A better
standard of living is a common motivation and reward for
people starting any kind of business. Money—and what it
can buy—is the universally recognizable indicator of
success that distributors use to motivate and establish
credibility for their business. Eventually, each person
defines what true success means to them. Beyond that,
people build an Amway business—or any business, really—
to satisfy many different needs. Not all relate to money or
material benefit. For example, people become Amway
distributors to sharpen their business skills or learn how to
own and operate their own company. Others want the
freedom to develop a business on their own time, at their
own pace. Some want to expand their network of friends
and business contacts, while others merely want the
satisfaction that comes from being around so many
optimistic, positive-thinking people.*

I've heard rumors that Amway is a cult. Is this true?

*No, Amway Corporation is a business and, similar to other
large and established companies, has a distinct environment defined by shared business goals. Shared business
philosophies should not be misinterpreted as a cult. Amway
offers a business opportunity that is open to all, regardless of religious beliefs, race or gender. Amway really is
a microcosm of the world, with more than 3 million
entrepreneurs worldwide representing nearly every culture,
ethnic background, and political and religious belief finding
in the Amway business a way to meet their goals. While
unique as individuals, Amway distributors share a desire to
succeed in a business of their own and recognize Amway as an
excellent opportunity to achieve their goals. New distri-*

butors receive training, motivation and support in building independent businesses, and are rewarded for their
achievements. A close look at Amway will reveal that any
reference to Amway as a cult is incorrect.

What is the difference between Amway and illegal pyramids?

Unlike illegal pyramids, Amway and other legitimate direct
sellers:

• Don't charge expensive fees to join, and refund most
or all start-up costs within a reasonable period if a person
decides to get out of the business. Many pyramids charge
exorbitant start-up fees and, even if they claim to offer a
refund, often don't honor that promise. To become an
Amway distributor, you only purchase an Opportunity Kit
(in the U.S. this costs less than $175), which costs far less
than most other business opportunities. What's more, the
cost of the Opportunity Kit is refundable should you decide
to leave the business for any reason.

• Pay no commissions or bonuses unless products are
sold. Amway does not pay bonuses for the mere act of
recruiting another person into the business. Pyramids, in
contrast, often do.

• Have no requirements to stock and maintain large,
expensive inventories. There are no minimum order require ments. Amway operates convenient, centrally located
warehouses and has excellent ordering and delivery programs so our distributors don't bear the expense or head-
ache of maintaining large inventories.

• Cover all products with ample Satisfaction Guarantees
so that customers and distributors may get most, if not all,
of their money back if they are unsatisfied for any reason.
(Pyramid schemes that plan only to operate for a couple
of months might offer a meaningless guarantee.)

Finally, pyramid schemes typically operate for a few months before they ultimately collapse and disappear. Amway, however, has been in business for nearly 40 years.

Does Amway really give people more free time, or does it require a lot of time to succeed?
Like any small business, it takes hard work to succeed in the Amway business, and that requires time and commitment, especially in the beginning. Our research shows that most people understand this very well. But the Amway business does offer flexibility for our distributors in running their business. Unlike most conventional jobs, Amway distributors can work at home, when they want, at their own pace, on their own schedule, according to the goals they have set for themselves. For some, that means if they need an afternoon to attend a school play, play golf, or see a friend, they can arrange their work schedule to allow this. The choice of when, where, and how much time to devote to their Amway business is theirs alone. This flexibility is one important reason why the opportunity appeals to so many people around the world.

CHAPTER SIX

Commitment to Excellence

During my early hands-on training program at Amway there was a learning experience to be had in every department I worked in. For instance, in Research and Development, I got to see the value of committing to a vision, taking initiative, and persevering. I found it interesting that while R and D had excellent scientists on the payroll, many good ideas came out of the mailbags full of letters from distributors, homemakers, and other users of our products. These letters contained ideas on everything from cosmetic applicators to electrical generators. Distributors and customers still send us letters. They write because they know that our company respects their concerns, listens to their ideas, and is committed to excellence in all that we do.

As a result of that commitment to excellence, I became aware of the increasing role that technology would play in the future of our expanding company. I learned that automation didn't replace people; it set them free to concentrate on tasks that were less repetitive and more intellectually stimulating and productive. In fact, by remaining compet-

*itive through automation, the business grew so much that
Amway had to hire even more people to keep up with demand.*

*In a very important part of my management training,
[my wife] Betty and I also became Amway distributors, experiencing firsthand how the values of the manufacturing
company translated from the plant floor into the homes and
lives of our distributors and customers. I saw that the quality of our products had a direct impact on the lives and
environment of the people who used them.*

—*Dick DeVos,* Rediscovering American Values

IN THE EXCERPT given above from his 1997 *New York
Times* bestseller Dick DeVos, president of Amway, focuses
on one of the major strong points in the company's business
perspective: **commitment to excellence.** This policy was,
in fact, the title and theme of Amway's first authorized
history book, published in 1986. And it is echoed again and
again in Jay Van Andel's autobiography, *An Enterprising
Life.*

Does the Act Live Up to the Assurance?

Many companies coin slogans that sound enticing when
used in advertising or on product packaging. But when you
get right down to it, the words are just so many clever little
bubbles of expression, without any real meaning in terms
of quality or service. In an essay entitled ''The Quality of
Excellence,'' in the book *Choices with Clout*, sums it up
with these words, ''People think in terms of excellence,
including success, wealth, achievements and gracious living. We feel uncomfortable about things at the lower end
of the scale. We become anxious about peoples and nations

in the grip of poverty. It makes us uneasy and often guilty to think of starving children and then realize what bounties we have in America. Yet we should always bear in mind that poor people cannot help other poor people. What we can do, however, is to condition ourselves to speak out and stand up for those things in which we believe. To do this effectively, we must first have faith—faith in self, faith in God, faith in our convictions. Once these conditions are met, you will be amazed at how easy it is to speak out.''

The attainment of excellence usually requires sacrifice, Van Andel counsels in the essay. ''You have to give up certain pleasures in order to devote time and effort to goals with higher priorities. . . . Some form of sacrifice exists in respect to almost everything of any consequence that people want to achieve. We have stated in a number of ways that success breeds success and excellence breeds excellence. This assertion is based on the proven fact that people who are successful continue to be so because they realize they can be successful and because they are committed to giving up certain things in order to attain excellence.''

Despite the attention paid to excellence, cautions Van Andel, ''the quality of excellence in America may really be on the decline. Why? Largely because people lack the faith that they can rise above mediocrity. In our society, power blocks have developed in which multitudes of people are trying to do the least and get the most for as little action as possible, and with minimal effort. . . .

''Are you going to settle for mediocrity or strive for excellence? The choice is yours.''

Dr. Robert Schuller, the noted theologian and author, and a longtime friend of Amway and believer in its work ethic, expressed it this way in a talk to distributors: ''The qualities of peoples' lives are in direct proportion to their commitment to excellence.'' He used as an illustration an image of concentric circles, like a paper target on a rifle range, each circle getting smaller and smaller and focusing in the center, which is labeled YOU. The concept here is to enlarge your horizons and your personal strength by taking advantage of broader existing strengths and having faith in each of them individually and all of them collectively. Ranging from the outer circle to the innermost, there are six basic faiths you can choose to help build your inner strength:

1. *Faith in Faith.* You can gain strength through belief in a higher power, no matter what your religious beliefs may be.

2. *Faith in America.* The strength of the nation in global affairs can impart its power directly to you if you identify yourself as a believer in the American heritage.

3. *Faith in Free Enterprise.* Identity with the system that has been, since the nation's founding, the key to success and excellence for those who believe in it.

4. *Faith in Community.* Whether you live in a rural village or a great metropolis, identify with the neighborhood in which you live and be a part of its activities and growth.

5. *Faith in Family.* Whether you belong to a large family or simply have a handful of relatives, take pride in your heritage.

6. *Faith in Yourself.* Lastly, but most importantly, believe in yourself and your own commitment to excellence and accomplishment.

Rich DeVos and Jay Van Andel have pointed out repeatedly that they have, over the years, talked to many hundreds of prospective distributors who expressed uncertainty about their abilities to be successful in Amway. "I'm just an ordinary kind of person, an average citizen," is a typical response. "What is so special about me that suggests a potential for real achievement?"

Their response: Every individual is unique and special. There is a wealth of good in every person whom God has placed in the world. That good needs only to be discovered, realized, and translated into action through inspiration and motivation.

In Search of Excellence

In its literature, speeches, and presentations to distributors and those being recruited, Amway has asked this question almost since the beginning of its history: *What do you do to choose a richer, more meaningful life? How do you pry yourself out of your shell? What do you do to enjoy your present or future job or be better at it or to be happier in what you are doing?*

Amway's answer is found in the most valuable gift you can give a person: encouragement to believe. Too many people say *can't.* They can't sell. They can't speak in public. They haven't had the right training or education to tackle some venture. When people are convinced that they cannot do something, then no matter how much you teach them or provide the details and counsel for achievement, they refuse to try. They have already said to themselves, "Well, I can't do that."

And thus they remain at a sublevel of existence, and are never likely to commit themselves to excellence.

If people are not motivated or are skeptical, then they

underestimate themselves, and all the details of a job become problems. They cannot undertake certain jobs or accomplish things because they have never done them before and never had any successes to give them confidence. But if people have faith, believe in what they are doing, and are motivated, then they will figure out the details.

The Amway philosophy of success has always pinpointed the belief that there are two types of individuals: those who believe they are victims of circumstances and those who believe they control circumstances. The controllers, the ones who have faith and who believe in themselves, make things happen. The key is to do it *now.* "It is often interesting to see what happens when people choose to make things happen," says a distributor training manual. "Too many people operate in an atmosphere of thinking that they are being put upon by others, so they do nothing. These people are always waiting for the right time for something to happen. Many men and women have been reared in an atmosphere that encourages people to wait for the right circumstances. But people who succeed do not wait for something to happen—they *make it happen!* When you choose to make something happen, you change the circumstances. You decide what to do. It does not matter which side of the bed you actually got up on or how you happened to feel when you woke up. Conditions are never perfect for getting on with something. People say they are too young or too old or too something else. If you don't choose to get around to doing something, it's because you have not yet learned the discipline of controlling the circumstances."

Amway's concept of the work ethic is that motivation provides the energy and faith serves as the compass for people who want to strive for excellence, not necessarily at an unrealistic and elevated level, but within the comfortable confines of their own competency and personal goals. People who consolidate their faith will always be the better for it.

Attitudes also play an important part in this philosophy of success. Few people will argue with the assertion that a positive attitude is a vital ingredient for the development of a rewarding career. But there should be no cutoff point. Throughout life, people need a positive, hopeful outlook in order to cope and to be effective. Self-doubt leads to disappointment and defeat.

"America has traditionally been a nation that fostered positive attitudes," Rich DeVos has said time and again. "Can you imagine where we would be today if it had been otherwise? Who would ever have chosen to venture out West with all the dangers and unknown circumstances that the early pioneers faced? Who would have had the temerity to form a new nation and take on the gargantuan problems of our government? Who would have wanted to found fledgling companies and industries or labor from dawn to dusk to grow crops? Or speak out against oppression in the face of vengeful enemies? Fortunately, today we can be more secure in making such choices, no matter how controversial, because we can look back on the documented records of others who have done so. We can, in effect, have the courage of our convictions."

The Relationship of Excellence and Motivation

A commitment to excellence, in the company's tradition, is directly linked to motivation. And motivation starts with a hunger, a need. The desire for money is not a bad motivation, but it is only a symbol for other motivational forces, such as the desire to improve one's lifestyle, living standards, environment, or education. Security is another motivating goal. And so also is independence, along with certain ego satisfactions. A sense of recognized personal accomplishment can be very satisfying for some people, even more so than money or material things. This is especially true when the motivation leads to voluntary public service, where the financial rewards are nonexistent or very modest.

There is a certain type of motivation called "reverse motivation," best illustrated perhaps by the rags-to-riches stories of people who were determined to escape the slums in which they spent their childhood. But Amway has always looked at motivation as a *positive* force, one that helps its people by making them believe in themselves and head for a constructive target rather than an escape from pain and distress. Most importantly, under this concept, distributors must believe in themselves. They can create an atmosphere of confidence in two ways: (1) by surrounding themselves with positive input and (2) by removing themselves from negative thoughts. They are taught to develop an awareness of the attitudes of those people with whom they are in constant contact, to avoid the ones who are always carping about the faults of others, who are professional complainers, and to ignore the assertions of people in business who tend to be cutthroat and self-serving. Always look forward, not back. As a golf pro once explained this, "a golfer who looks back at his last bad shot is just going to hit another bad shot. Never dwell on what went wrong, but only on what you are doing that is right."

Distributors are urged to follow the Jeffersonian interpretation of leaders as ones "who not only lead but who teach others how to lead." In fact, this leadership role is the heart and substance of the whole tradition of building business by constantly developing and working with new leaders.

Positivism Versus Negativism

In their training progams, seminars, rallies, and other basic communications activities, distributors have learned over the years and down through the handing of leadership from one generation to the next to "accentuate the positive." This outlook is seen, for example, in the selection of materials for study and self-improvement. In today's world, it is not always easy to read, see, or hear about something that will inspire us. We are so bombarded with information from all sides that trying to select what we want to read, see, or hear becomes a greater problem than ever before in the history of communication. The media keep proliferating. In addition to the few basic forms that brought messages to our parents and grandparents, we now have television, audiocassettes, e-mail, the Internet, videotapes, message recorders, dozens of new types of phone devices, and endless ways of speeding up dialogues almost to the point of frenzy, not to mention the seemingly limitless capacities of the computer to add to the input and output. As successful distributors tell people they are recruiting, the pursuit of excellence can be achieved only when they discipline themselves to tune in the positive dialogues and tune out the negative ones. The choices are made somewhat easier in light of the fact that there are probably only one-tenth as many media messages on the positive side as there are on the negative. Thus, they can weed out a great mass of garbage before they even start the selection process.

Reading is advocated as important because it is personal and can be done at one's own pace, in an environment that encourages reflection and a more considered evaluation of facts and opinions. Very few people can cope with television as a means of orderly communication—not when so many, many messages are being thrust at them rapid-fire, and often in helter-skelter fashion. One of the greatest challenges in recruitment programs has been for their mentors to overcome those in their audiences who are skeptical and cite the easily available statistics about the number of companies, large and small, that go bankrupt, have to sell out, or cease operations. "How do I know I won't expend a lot of time and effort," they ask, "and then see this happen to me?" One answer of course is that what happens in most cases is that these companies are forced out of business because their managers failed to realize the changes taking place in time to take corrective action. And Amway has long had a reputation for training people to study and anticipate such changes and be prepared.

The bottom line is that a commitment to excellence is a commitment to learning.

A Lifetime Achievement

"Opportunity comes to each one of us several times in our lifetime, but it's our choice what we do and what decisions we make about these opportunities," said Amway Crown Ambassador Birdie Yager before an audience of several thousand cheering distributors. "You have to believe that what you're doing is right."

She said this on the occasion when she and her husband, Dexter, received the Lifetime Achievement Award from the Multilevel Marketing Association for their achievements during their long career as Amway distributors. They had started from scratch in 1964, after Dexter had looked into, and several times turned down, an Amway opportunity. By the time they received the MMA honor, they had built up an organization of what *Forbes* magazine estimated conservatively as 100,000 distributors. Although the exact number was never publicized, the MMA stated in its acclamation: "The Yagers have more active distributors in their own downline than the total number of active distributors in many successful networking companies combined."

How did they achieve this degree of excellence in their careers? On the last page of his book, *Millionaire Mentality,* Dexter lists what he calls the "five Keys to Success": dreams, attitude, work, proper vehicle, and duplication.

"There's some point in your business when you've got to get it all together," says Dexter, "where it is more than just a pin and some dollars, but it represents the heart of America, the dream of America, until it represents the American people. It represents someone else's life that you're out there striving to help make it, instead of just you making it."

Acting out of love and concern for others is a major part of the Yager philosophy. "Today, when people don't trust people, you and I can show them that we're trustworthy. Today, when love is needed more than ever, we've got a chance to say 'I love you.' People need people. And those who fill that need get paid well. But you have to look at something beyond the money. You've got to look at the excitement of helping somebody else."

Known as the master dreambuilder, Dexter frequently underlines the need for each of us to build a meaningful dream that we can believe in. "Get your dream tank filled," he says. "There's an old song that says 'If you don't have a dream, how ya' gonna have a dream come true?' And you've got to believe in your dream."

What is the quality of success? According to Dexter, "Success is the progressive realization of a worthwhile dream. Real success is not to be taken for granted. The achievement of our goals, if of value to begin with, is no minor undertaking. If you do not have to work to accomplish a goal, then probably there was no validity to it in the first place. Anything of value is worth exerting the effort to obtain. One underlying fact always must remain: A dream unrealized is a dream imprisoned by that enemy of all enemies—the fear of failure. Set that dream free by determining that you will make it happen."

Free Enterprise

The question arises: It is all well and good for Amway to be committed to excellence in its corporate operations, the products it manufactures, and its policies for the company's twelve to fourteen thousand employees, but what about the distributors? If they are independent, as described, and personally responsible for the way they do business, how is the Amway concept of "excellence" made practicable and procedural in their daily operations in widely dispersed parts of the globe?

The answer is that Amway strongly promotes the American free enterprise concept, which in itself is dedicated to excellence in business and commercial enterprises, through both inspiration and the insistence on professional integrity. At the core of the Amway philosophy lies a strong belief in the virtues and benefits of free enterprise, which has long fostered the company's success and must be preserved if future generations of businesspeople are to enjoy the same opportunities. Most importantly, the interpretation of the philosophy is a basic, down-to-earth one, not a stuffy and complex rehash of intellectual economic theories.

It was recognized at the very start that Amway would bring a lot of people into the business world as entrepreneurs who had never thought of doing this before. That is, of course, the concept of free enterprise: being an independent entrepreneur and running your own ship, so to speak. All of these things are what attract people into the Amway business to begin with. "We decided early on," reflected Jay Van Andel, "that our cause goes beyond that of a simple, materialistic way of making money. The free enterprise system does not revolve around the General Motors Corporations of this world. It revolves around the small-business system. There are at least fifteen million small businesses in this country, such as gasoline stations, barber shops, hardware stores, grocery stores, bars, restaurants, and all those things, and basically these form the real core of the American free enterprise system. These small businesses are where it all starts, because every big business was once a small business, not something that dropped out of the sky full-blown."

Rich DeVos says in recollection, "Our involvement with free enterprise was really a step-by-step process. You know, we sat in the basement in the early years talking about the concept of Amway and the simple words came out that the idea of owning and operating our own business, of being rewarded in relationship to what we did, were just things we felt and believed in. We felt at the beginning that Amway needed to stand up for something, and the principles of free enterprise were the very foundations on which Amway was built."

As history has demonstrated, distributors are constantly perpetuating this concept of free enterprise and excellence, whether they realize it or not. When they sponsor new distributors, they put them in business and make them active participants in the system. That step attracts more converts to the concept of free enterprise than all the talking and reading and lecturing will ever do. They rise or fall, but they gain a new respect for what it takes to make a business run. From Amway's point of view, personal freedom springs from economic freedom. "Freedom and free enterprise are like Siamese twins," Van Andel once said. "One cannot live without the other. Allowing people the freedom to work for themselves and compete in a free marketplace has been the best, most productive economic approach ever devised."

Successful distributors have been echoing this outlook in their own personal comments for four decades. A good example is that of Double Diamonds Robb and Marilyn Tobey of Oregon. "We can be our own boss," they said. "We work extremely hard, but it's because we choose to do it—not because of some time clock. This freedom is very precious to us. It's what we want for our children. That's why the preservation of free enterprise and the Amway Sales and Marketing Plan are so important to us. It's not just the dollars, it's the quality of life that we've found."

This kind of excellence in living, as well as working, is a key point of inspiration and encouragement.

One of the exciting aspects of the Amway philosophy is that the free enterprise system, although usually interpreted as being typically American, works in other countries as well. Consider this comment from distributors Edward and Patria Silfa, working together in the Dominican Republic. "It's great to be the owners of our own business and learn the self-discipline that is required to develop it. What motivates us most in our Amway business is helping other people realize their own potential."

Amway, as a corporation, has always supported free enterprise as a concept that opposes government intervention in business beyond the minimum necessary to protect personal and property rights. As might be imagined, this attitude has not been popular with some politicians and bureaucrats, who would like to keep their claws on the business world. But founders and the present managers of Amway have always been willing to stick their necks out and have long opposed the flood of nit-picking regulations that stifle personal initiative and inflate the costs of doing business.

"In our free enterprise economic system," explains DeVos, "the businessman owns his own tools, risks his own money, sets his own price, reaches his own decisions, and makes or loses money depending upon how well he provides the public with a product or service it wants at a price it is willing to pay. Unless he does something criminal or violates the public interest, the government should leave him alone."

Amway's management frequently voices concerns that America seems to be moving away from free enterprise toward a socialistic system that increases government control over excellence and productivity. It is characteristic of the Amway philosophy as a way of life, and not simply the approach to a sales program, that this changing perspective prompted positive action. DeVos and Van Andel expressed alarm that economic instruction in schools was focusing much more on theory than on practice, and that students were seldom being taught that companies needed profits to pay salaries, expand, and even survive.

The voice of free enterprise rang loud and clear when independent distributors began to commemorate Free Enterprise Day each year with rallies across the country. In the mid-1990s, for example, the company helped to sponsor a gigantic "Spirit of America—Free Enterprise" rally in Atlanta, Georgia, that was attended by seventy-five thousand people.

In the 1990s, the concept of free enterprise, coupled with a commitment to excellence, began making substantial—if not historical—inroads in other countries as Amway opened its opportunities to more and more lands around the globe.

Fighting for Freedom

Free enterprise can be a sensitive, if not controversial, subject. Those who accept this system as a work ethic and promoter of business excellence discover that success inevitably attracts scrutiny, and not always the beneficial kind. Almost since its founding, Amway had endured accusations that it was fostering a "pyramid" scheme, whereby participants made their profits by signing up salespeople, with the newest recruits left holding the bag. Public concern grew as a number of fraudulent schemes were exposed and, in 1969, the Federal Trade Commission (FTC) began to investigate several companies, Amway and Nutrilite among them. Six years later, a formal complaint was issued to Amway. Two more years passed as company attorneys wrestled with the FTC in efforts to determine what charges would be made, what depositions should be taken, what documents were required, and how to prepare for the forthcoming hearings.

A three-month-long hearing began in May 1977. Then, after nearly a year of deliberation, the administrative law judge rendered his decision: Most of the charges were dismissed. Equally important, the judge made the same determination the full Federal Trade Commission subsequently reported: *"We have determined that the Amway Sales and Marketing Plan is not an illegal 'pyramid scheme'; that the non-price-related rules Amway has imposed on the distributors of its products, to control the way products flow to consumers, do not constitute unreasonable restraints of trade or unfair methods of competi-*

tion; and that, with the exception of certain earnings claims, respondents [Amway's officers] have not made false, misleading, or deceptive claims about Amway's business or the opportunities it presents to a person who becomes part of it.''

This landmark ruling finally cleared the air.

Can You Dream, yet Still Be Committed to Excellence?

In his many talks to Amway distributors, Dr. Shad Helmstetter presents what he calls "the positive power of dreambuilding," which he states is "one of the most important reasons why Amway is successful."

At first sight, this might seem like the common practice of wishful thinking—knowing what other people with more money and/or capabilities might have and then dreaming about how you too could have them. The fact of the matter is, however, that this procedure is a skill that has to be learned, practiced, and put into action. "The first thing about dreambuilding," says Helmstetter, "is that you have to learn how to do it. It doesn't come naturally." That is where Amway comes in—it shows its distributors how to build dreams, by providing guidelines anyone can follow, demonstrating how to practice the art, and perfecting the application on a daily basis.

Dreambuilding is the perfection of excellence. Or, as Helmstetter tells his audience, "Dreambuilding is seeing yourself living a life of quality and substance—choosing where you live, choosing what you do, and choosing *your* future for yourself." It is a way to control what you *think,* to enhance what you *believe,* and to solidify your *attitude.*

BE AN ATTITUDE EXPERT

As you probably are discovering, the Amway business is full of very positive people. But as with any endeavor, you will encounter those who have a negative attitude—either about your business or about life in general. Here are some suggestions to help you deal with this attitude.

One successful Diamond offers this advice: "I used to be very confrontational with people when they started talking negatively to me about the business, and I would try to argue with them. But now I do something totally unexpected: I agree with them! I say something like, 'I know just how you feel because I felt exactly the same way before I really knew what it was all about.' It always seems to surprise people to hear this and then they are more willing to listen to what I have to say."

An Emerald says she has discovered many people who have negative attitudes on the outside "have wonderful attitudes on the inside. They have just been beaten down so much by the wrong lifestyle, the wrong job, or the wrong boss, that their real personality is buried."

Sometimes, she has found, negative people turn out to be the best prospects of all because they are the ones who are looking for something else in life. "They know they are unhappy, but they do not know what to do about it," she says. How do you turn that negative into a positive? By showing them that you have the vehicle that really can change their lives. You can offer them hope when they feel as though they are in a hopeless situation. Best of all, there are no limits on those you can help. Anyone can start an Amway business, regardless of education, experience, marital, or social status. And that is one of the most positive aspects of your business.

There is no greater feeling in the world than helping another human being—seeing the "sparkle" come back into their eyes, and the smiles return to their faces. With your positive attitude and belief in your business, you can make it happen for many people, even those who seem to be the most negative.

—Excerpted from a recent *Special Newsletter for New Distributors*

THE QUALITY OF EXCELLENCE

People think in terms of excellence, including success, wealth achievements, and gracious living. We feel uncomfortable about things at the lower end of the scale. We become anxious about peoples and nations in the grip of poverty. It makes us uneasy and often guilty to think of starving children and realize what bounties we have in America. Yet we should always bear in mind that poor people cannot help other poor people. What we can do, however, is to condition ourselves to speak out and stand up for those things in which we believe. To do this effectively, we must first have faith— faith in self, faith in God, faith in our convictions. Once these conditions are met, you will be amazed at how easy it is to speak out.

Success usually requires sacrifice. You have to give up certain pleasures in order to devote time and effort to goals with higher priorities. Are you ready now?

Despite the attention paid to excellence, the quality of excellence may really be on the decline. Why? Largely because people lack the faith that they can rise above mediocrity. In our society, power blocks have developed in which multitudes of people are trying to do the least and get the most for as little action as possible and with minimal effort.

We have to counter this by understanding how we can do more in order to get more, how we can escalate a faith in ourselves and a belief in our own worth to attain much higher goals in life. By doing so, we restore the whole concept of America and how it was developed through a striving for excellence on the part of our forefathers.

There is a strange and inexplicable trend today to apologize for success and to proclaim poverty and nonachievement as virtues. Being low key is the in thing these days, even if it seems to be nothing more than doing nothing.

Are you going to settle for mediocrity or strive for excellence? The choice is yours. Do you want to achieve things or simply line up a few perks, such as minimal expenses for entertaining or the use of a personal car?

Many people equate success in terms of status, preferring to be the captain of a small ship rather than one of many officers on an ocean liner. They feel—although it is not always true—that they will get more recognition on the one hand and avoid much of the tediousness on the other hand. Linking yourself to community provides this "small ship" atmosphere because, even though the community is an urban one or quite large, the people who volunteer are likely to hold informal, even amateur, standings.

Working in community, you are also likely to encounter a good many people who are older, looking for a purpose in life, or lonely. As we said earlier, if you want to move a lot of people in a certain direction, locate the lonely individuals of this world and offer them something that will counteract their isolation. Most people have certain feelings of loneliness, even if they are relatively secure in a family or group. This sometimes translates into a feeling that they lack some kind of recognition they had hoped for—rather than simply being physically isolated from other people. So one form of motivation is the need to combat this void in peoples' lives.

—Excerpted from *Choices with Clout: How to Make Things Happen by Making the Right Decisions Every Day of Your Life*, by Wilbur Cross, based on interviews with Rich DeVos and Jay Van Andel

When applied to business, dreambuilding can help in three ways:

1. Providing a mental computer that can be programed with positive instructions that lead to success.

2. Forcing the "dreamer" to make specific choices about the essentials that are important, both in a career and in a lifestyle.

3. Getting people both to set goals and to have the earnest desire to achieve them.

During this educational program, participants learn the "Self-Talk" principle, which heads dreams in the right direction, establishes positive mental insights, and results in beneficial habits that become part of one's daily life.

CHAPTER SEVEN

People Power: Domestic Growth in North America

The typical Amway success story is that of the housewife, who starts distributing Amway products on a part-time basis, is successful enough so that her husband, tired of his nine-to-five job, joins her and together they go on to developing a successful new business. Yet there are many cases of people who decided to try their hand as independent business owners and distributors of Amway products, but who then gave up and went back to their old jobs. Paul Miller is a good example. He tried and quit the Amway business in despair, but later tried all over again, and the second time around achieved great success.

"I was given a kit," he explains about his original failed attempt, "but nothing more. I didn't even know where the products came from."

This was unusual for a man who had enjoyed many successful ventures in his life. While in college as an undergraduate, he had won an award for courage when, sidelined by a serious back injury, he fought his way to become starting quarterback at the University of North Carolina.

Reflecting the same tremendous drive, he was enrolled in master's programs for both law and business administration in 1974, when a friend showed him the real potential of the Amway Sales and Marketing Plan.

The first person he sponsored was Debbie, the young lady he was destined to marry.

"Paul and I dated in college," she said. "After graduation, I taught school, and after about three and a half years of dating Paul, I was ready to get married. But I felt Paul was paying more attention to the business than to me. However, the Amway business was good for Paul. He saw happily married couples working together, and that made him ready for marriage.

"And Amway helped Paul become happier with himself. He only became a lawyer because he couldn't pass chemistry to become a dentist." She smiles.

"For sixteen months, we really stumbled around in this business," says Paul, grinning. "We thought Amway was great, but we were scared to call people and afraid of getting rejected. We'd go to rallies, but we didn't do any work between rallies."

"Then we went to an Amway function where everything just came to light," says Debbie. "We saw that Amway wasn't just a soap business, and that people's lives were changed. It made us proud to be in the Amway business.

"After that, we started getting bold and calling people, and that's the key! We called people we were scared of—people who were doing much better than us financially. But now we knew we had something special to offer them.

"And they were the ones who were the most interested—the ones who were self-motivated and ready to take off. Paul sponsored five in a row after we'd been in sixteen

months with almost no results. Six months later, we were Directs."

"Many successful people have reached dead ends in their careers," explains Paul. *"Then they consider Amway, and learn how the Plan will let them use their success skills."*

"They didn't look at the old car we were driving or the small apartment we were living in," adds Debbie. *"Nine of our Direct legs are people we contacted when we were living in student housing and had nothing but excitement to offer. They knew we believed in this business. So it's not the material things you've acquired that will make or break your business."*

As they pointed out, when people become Direct Distributors, they can choose between spending their increased income on extras or investing it in their business. So they used it to meet more people and increase their potential for the future. In the long run it worked, and not only gave them more opportunities, but made it possible to improve their lifestyle and at the same time enjoy being with their three children more often, and doing the things they liked to do.

—*Adapted from* Amagram *interviews*

"THE KEY TO AMWAY is its people," says an introductory statement in the official Amway history, *Commitment to Excellence,* coauthored by the author of this book and published by the Benjamin Company in 1986. "Ask someone who is close to the company and its organization to describe Amway and this is one of the themes that will be emphasized. The enthusiasm and *esprit de corps* of those who elect careers with Amway command universal recognition outside of the company as well as within."

No history of Amway would be complete without a few
case histories of successful distributors and how they were
able to achieve their goals. The following examples are
presented here for the purpose of providing readers with
this kind of information. However, these are simply the
author's selections from several hundred that have appeared
in the Amway magazine, *Amagram*—and which in turn
were selected from the many thousands that are similar in
degree in the matter of accomplishment, and should not be
construed as being the "best" or the most meritorious.

Turnaround from Adversity

Ed Johnson is no stranger to success. A master of
achievement born with business in his blood, he produces
a profile that reads like a who's who of accomplishment.
His biography lists achievements in finance, real estate, and
the presidency of one of the most prestigious law firms in
San Antonio, Texas. But Ed is no stranger to adversity,
either. During a period in the mid-1980s, when the recession hit Texas hard, he found himself caught in the middle.

"When the Texas economy went down the drain," Ed
reflects, "so did we." Suffice it to say, he and his wife,
Yvonne, lost literally everything, including their expensive
home, luxury cars, and many of their personal things of
value.

Yvonne, who along with Ed had become accustomed to
their affluent lifestyle, went back to work to help support the
family. And Ed basically started all over again. Today,
they're back in business together. Even more remarkable,
however, is what has happened to the Johnson family during
their journey.

Ed had been an Amway distributor in college in 1965
and again in 1978—both times without Yvonne. But it

wasn't until his son, Michael, showed Ed the Amway Sales and Marketing Plan in 1992 that he did anything with it. Now, their daughter Hilary is a distributor as well, and another daughter, Megan, lends support to the business.

"Apparently I'm the secret," Yvonne laughs. Ed enthusiastically agrees. It wasn't always a laughing matter for Yvonne, though. "I was not the least bit excited about it at first," she admits. "We were still in the recovery mode from our financial collapse, and I didn't need one more disaster. My dreams had been shot down—they were gone."

Still, she supported Ed as he tried to rethink his goals and shape his life in a different pattern. Together, they picked up the shattered pieces and rebuilt their lives. "It's necessary to build this business with a sense of urgency and passion and to build it with persistence, consistency, and commitment," Ed says.

For the Johnson family, they unexpectedly faced even greater crises than before. During the period when he was qualifying for Diamond, Ed had to face urgent surgery to remove a brain tumor, following a series of splitting migraine headaches. He underwent radiation therapy, but during his recovery in the hospital, he showed his mettle and his desire to get on with his life by prospecting three doctors and six nurses. With these successes, the Johnsons went Diamond—sixty-two months after signing on.

Although Ed's health challenges would have devastated most families, the Johnsons saw them as an opportunity to pull together. "There are no excuses," Ed says, "just performance!"

In addition to his law practice, Ed handles a share of the Amway business part-time, while Yvonne works full-time. Together, they present the Amway Sales and Marketing Plan in the evenings. Saturdays are reserved for the busi-

ness, which is run out of a glassed-in office set between the
kitchen and music room of their Spanish colonial–style
home. The office overlooks a pool area and more than sixty
stately old oak trees scattered throughout a heavily wooded
lot, where squirrels and doves greet the family each day.

"We are truly an Amway family," Ed asserts with
gusto. "It is our life, we have fun with it, and all of our
best friends are involved in it because we've brought them
in, too. It's like one big happy family. We love it!"

Quarterbacking for Amway

Back in the 1970s, Tim Foley was the idol of Miami
Dolphin fans, especially when, in 1972, as a quarterback,
he helped the team to a perfect 17–0 season. But Tim knew,
as all professional athletes do, that his production time was
limited and he eventually had to set other goals for the
future. For Tim and his wife, Connie, it meant to start at
something new. Amway was their choice, and Tim, putting
his glory days behind him, accepted the fact that he would
have to withstand, at the start, the humility of being a nov-
ice.

"When we got started in the business," he admits, "I
wasn't too open to suggestions. There I was, a Northerner,
urban raised, while my upline was from a small town in
North Carolina. I was a little arrogant. I thought, 'If he can
be successful, I know I can.' But it soon became apparent
there was a major difference between us: He had money,
and I was broke. I soon realized if I were going to be
successful, I'd have to shut up and listen. Fortunately, my
upline was patient with me."

Tim never forgot those early lessons. "Often people
make judgments based on an individual's educational background," he says. "But as you build the business, you learn

not to do that. Though many professional people build extremely successful Amway businesses, a doctor or businessman won't necessarily apply himself here. And a person with no glimmer of success in the past can become very successful. When you see that happen, the initial evaluation you might make about someone disappears. You learn this through experience."

Until then, Connie had been a homemaker. "I was no businesswoman," she recalls. "My personal challenge was coming out of my comfort zone, which was being home with the children. I had to develop my people skills, my leadership skills. Just like being pregnant, it's not always fun, but you want the results."

Today, with her warm personality, she loves working with people, and her business associates have become her closest friends. "Tim's not the guru, and I'm not the matriarch," she insists, adding that over the next couple of days they'll be hosting Emeralds at their home, where they'll spend two days "talking, relaxing, not dressing up in suits or gowns—just listening to where they are, their challenges, what's working and what's not."

"I like to have fun," Connie admits. "I can think of moments when I was just ecstatic with joy. Like the time we were skiing in the mountains. I stood there, admiring the beauty, but staring down the steep hill, and afraid to move. Then I heard my kids, who once looked to me for courage, say encouragingly, 'You can do it, Mom!' And I did."

With tears in her eyes, she says, "I've learned to look for those moments that are wonderful. I don't have a lot of excuses to be in a bad mood."

"At that point," Tim reflects, glancing down at the massive Super Bowl ring that today is the only visible reminder of his NFL days, "I decided that if being an Amway dis-

tributor was what God was condemning me to be, I'd try
to suffer merrily."

"It was a hard time for me," said Connie soberly, who,
despite her natural optimism, feared she and Tim would
never attain the life they dreamed of for Kate and Tommy,
then only seven and three. "At one point, I had to cash in
the kids' savings bonds to pay off a debt. I felt terrible
about it. On my way home from the bank, I had a flat tire.
I remember standing there, looking at the tire, and I just
wanted to quit."

Later in life, with Kate married and working in her parents' business and Tommy away at college, Tim and Connie could well have led a life of ease. Instead, they sat down
at the kitchen table together and outlined their goals and
plans. They continue to work hard, achieving the top levels
of Crown and Crown Ambassador in 1997. Why did they
do it? Why didn't they stop at Triple Diamond or, if that
wasn't enough, at Crown?

With the competitive spirit of the athlete, Tim says simply, "We did it because it was there." It's second nature
to him. "If something is a possibility, you work toward
that possibility," he adds, as though to do otherwise is not
an option. The second critical factor, Tim points out, is that
he and Connie are motivated by the outstanding examples
from everyone in their upline. He mentioned several names:
Steve and Annette Woods, Bill Childers, Hal and Susan
Gooch, and the example Dexter and Birdie Yager had set
for them for so many years.

In the beginning, money was the motivator because they
were desperate. Later, it became secondary. "Much more
important were the friendships, the things you learn, the
team," said Tim. In many ways, he likened this to his experience with the Miami Dolphins. "In 1972, they called
us the 'no-name' defense—eleven guys who worked to-

gether to win the Super Bowl and didn't care who got the credit. We were individually anonymous but collectively very effective. You can apply that same philosophy to this business. There are a lot of unsung heroes. When I see someone with rough hands, dirt under his fingernails, calluses, and he attends meetings in a borrowed suit, I can learn from him. I can learn about courage from people who have overcome serious illness and big debt. That's what this business is all about.

"To be successful in Amway requires a balance between selling and sponsoring. It's a people business that gives people the opportunity to create a new life for themselves."

Putting Disaster on Hold

What do most people do when a flood, tornado, earthquake, or other violent force of nature all but destroys their homes, their businesses, and their way of life?

Most people spend weeks, months, and perhaps years grieving, floundering, and struggling to get back to even a semblance of normalcy. During this period, family affairs are disrupted, remunerative work grinds to a halt, social events are bypassed, and the victims seem to be subjected to endless amounts of time-consuming paperwork and marathon phone calls in panicky attempts to place insurance claims and repair damages.

Not so in the case of Stuart and Edith Upchurch when Hurricane Fran struck their home in the Southern Piedmont region in 1996. When the storm abated, they saw nothing but total devastation around them and critical damage to their home. But, instead of wringing their hands and going into a complete funk, they took it in stride, arranged for temporary quarters for themselves and their Amway office, and remained determined to conduct "business as usual" during the period of rehabilitation.

This was quite an ambitious goal, given the fact that it required sixty dump-truck loads to clear the property of shattered trees, bushes, and other trash, not to mention almost $150,000 worth of repair to the property.

Still, that wasn't enough to deter them. Even as soon as the morning after the storm, Edith expressed her faith in the future by exclaiming, "Now I know we're going Diamond."

And, do you know, that is just what they did.

"This could have distracted us completely," Stuart said, "but we just wouldn't let it."

In fact, not much then or since has deterred them from pursuing their dream. Before they started their Amway business, Stuart and Edith were content—or so they thought. She was busy managing commercial real estate properties, while he managed a wholesale beverage distributorship. "We were climbing the ladder with vigor and success," Stuart recounted, "and making good money."

Yet the stress of corporate life, and the demands by others on their time, was taking its toll. "We started to see what *not* having time to spend with one another does to a relationship," Stuart says. Then in 1984, he met their would-be sponsor while on the job, and was impressed with his positive outlook, description of the business, and his compassion for other people. "Our personal relationship developed," Stuart explained, "and one day he asked me if I might be open to doing something else on the side."

Two years later, Stuart and Edith found themselves having to make a big decision. At that point, the company for which Stuart worked had a situation that forced him to choose between his job and their Amway business. "It really wasn't that difficult a decision to make," Stuart recalled later. "We were convinced our future lay in developing the Amway business. We chose a passion for freedom over a solid job," he adds.

Then, the going got really tough. For a period of time after leaving his job to keep building the Amway distributorship, Stuart had to start another enterprise—a gutter-cleaning service—just to help make ends meet.

Ultimately, their toil and patience paid off. Today both Stuart and Edith pursue their Amway goals full-time from their contemporary custom home—which they are still in the process of repairing. "We had a choice: focus on our Amway business and our future or fix the house. Again, we chose to follow our dream," Stuart says.

Although Stuart and Edith work hard, and although they had to make many sacrifices in time and recreation to put the hurricane disaster behind them, they're also doing what they love most—and which is made possible by having the kind of freedom Amway provides: traveling. "It's something Edith grew up doing and was unable to continue as an adult until now," Stuart said, noting the fact that an Amway business can be built almost anywhere in the world—and even when traveling for business, they make sure they allow time to relax. Says Stuart: "We both like to spend time in beautiful, quiet, peaceful places with good breezes and beautiful water." And as all their friends, relatives, and fellow distributors would agree, they certainly deserve it.

From an Ancient Heritage to a New One

Dan Yuen grew up with an example of dedication and persistence passed down to him from his father and mother. Faced with the prospect of continuing poverty and misery in his native China, Dan's father had emigrated alone, at the tender age of sixteen, to Canada. He started his new life in Victoria, where he found hourly jobs on local farms. Later, after workng hard at learning English, he moved to Vancouver and eventually opened his own grocery store.

As was common in China, Dan's parents had been brought together through an arranged marriage. "My mother had never met my father or even talked to him," explained Dan. "It was a total culture shock. She was so homesick she cried every night, but she had made a commitment, and it was for life."

Dan was much more fortunate. He was independent, able to seek and find the right spouse for himself; he married Sandy, and soon they had a son, Connor, and an attractive home in a suburb of Vancouver, British Columbia. There, the beautifully manicured lawns, carefully tended flower beds, and private, fenced-in backyards were in sharp contrast with the tough, run-down area in East Vancouver where Dan grew up, and with the poverty Sandy herself had experienced as a child on the Saskatchewan prairies.

Sandy's family had started out poor, and had become even poorer after her parents separated. Taking Sandy and her two sisters with her, Sandy's mother had set out on her own, with a dollar in her wallet. "We lived in one bedroom," said Sandy. "We three girls slept together in the one bed, while Mom slept on the couch."

Dan grins whenever he hears his wife's description of poverty on the plains. "If *we* had seen Sandy's family, their situation would have looked like wealth to us," Dan says with a laugh, recalling how hard his parents struggled just to put food on the table. He remembers seeing his mother fill a bowl of rice for his grandmother. To conceal the fact that there wasn't enough left for herself, his mother inverted a smaller bowl inside her own rice bowl, creating a false bottom. "My mother was a very giving person. She didn't want us to know she was going hungry so she could give a larger portion to my grandmother.''

If anything, the hardships they faced early in life made Dan and Sandy even more determined to succeed. As a teenager, Sandy worked hard to earn extra money. She cleaned houses until she got her driver's license, then found jobs cleaning bars, waiting on tables, and working in a store and a tuxedo shop. Many of her classmates left school after the eighth grade, but Sandy, determined to get an education to help lift her from her impoverishment, finished high school, then moved to Saskatoon and a job with a financing company. When Sandy met Dan, she was working as a sales representative for a financing firm in Vancouver. She'd been attracted to the job by assurances of a good salary and use of a company car, but she was soon disillusioned by the exorbitant demands on her time. After working twelve hours during the day, she was expected to entertain customers at nighttime hockey games and in bars. And she resented the unequal-treatment policy, under which, as she recalls, ''the men were paid more and treated better, even though I was training them and doing all the work. One of the things I was to appreciate, later, about the Amway business, was that if I worked as hard as a man, I could make as much money as a man.''

After college, Dan held a variety of positions with major corporations. He was working as a sales representative for a cellular phone company when his future Amway sponsor, a total stranger at the time, walked in the door and asked Dan if he was interested in looking at another business opportunity.

Dan started building his business in March 1988. By the third month, when he reached 4,000 PV (''Point Value,'' to designate accumulated product sales), he started dating Sandy, and, suddenly, business came to a grinding halt. ''I didn't show the Sales and Marketing Plan for about fifteen months,'' he recalls. "I was too busy courting my future wife.''

Almost a year had passed when, one day, Dan and Sandy took a hard look at their future, and Dan refocused his attention on his business. He got his stride and in April 1990 made Direct and by January 1991, Pearl. That month, he and Sandy were married, and the business really took off. They achieved Emerald that year, Diamond in 1992, and Executive Diamond in 1994.

Throughout this period, Dan and Sandy received solid support from their upline Diamonds, who helped them lay the foundation, and their upline Double Diamonds, who provided the leadership they needed to keep going when business was slack.

But rising this fast required sacrifices. Many times, Dan admits, he thought about quitting. Yet, despite misgivings by family and friends, he and Sandy had a burning desire to succeed. They have no doubt in their minds that every bit of time and effort they invested has been rewarded many times over.

Reflecting on qualities like perseverance and goal-setting, Dan refers to his boyhood, when he was often the target of racial taunts, and he fought back. "I had black eyes all the time,'' he recalls. This motivated him to enroll in karate instruction at age sixteen and later kung fu, a Chinese art of self-defense.

"In this business, a lot of people quit along the way,'' he observes. "My training in martial arts gave me the mental edge I needed. I had teeth knocked out, broken toes, broken ribs, but I never quit!'' He likes to draw a parallel between karate and the Amway business, based on distributors' use of the phrase "break a leg'' to refer to qualification of a downline Direct Distributor. Once, he explains, he accidentally broke the leg of an opponent. He visited the man in the hospital, and they became good friends. When Dan started his Amway business, this man was the first person he sponsored. The man eventually became Dan's sixth Direct—the one who gave him the required total for Diamond qualification. "Considering all the experience I had breaking legs in karate," he jokes, "it was good training for Amway."

"Joking aside," Dan concludes, "Sandy and I made a total commitment to build this business. Now we concentrate on providing the same kind of leadership we were fortunate enough to receive for the people in our own organization."

The Good Old Days

There are so many inspirational stories about the people—mainly couples—who joined Amway in its early years and helped to shape the future of the business that it is hard to single out any small number of them as models of what Amway can mean to people during an entire lifetime career. But here are some examples of a few who serve to represent the whole, and what they have to say about what Amway has meant to them. They are presented in alphabetical order, as the most equitable manner of introducing them.

Bill and Peggy Britt

Although Bill earned an engineering degree and was a city manager in Raleigh, North Carolina, for fifteen years, his career left something to be desired. "I got to work early," he reminisces, "stayed late, always did more work than anyone could expect of me—and all it got me was poverty." Although his wife, Peggy, supplemented their income by working for the Carolina Power and Light Company, they faced a financial problem in 1970 when one of their investments failed. They had to make a major change in their careers—and it turned out to be the best of all decisions for them: to go with Amway. Today, as Crown Ambassadors, their achievements place them at the highest level in the business. Typical of those who become leaders in their field, he adds, ''The most vital thing we do is educate people about how to own and operate their own successful business. You can only temporarily build a business on emotion and excitement. We take knowledge we learned the hard way and give it to our people.'' (Incidentally, his ''people'' include thousands of Amway distributors all around the globe!)

George and Ruth Halsey

Many years ago, when Amway was still a fledgling business, George Halsey was a stock clerk in a shoe store in the Bronx, a borough of New York City, and his wife, Ruth, was a housewife with two children on her hands. In 1975, they joined Amway to make a little extra money to pay mounting bills. Because they were black, they might easily have been discouraged by comments from neighbors and acquaintances that minority people stood little chance to make good in this kind of selling. ''But the more often people told us that blacks can't make it in the Amway business,'' says Ruth, ''the harder we worked. We were determined to prove those statements false.'' They did just that—and much more (see page 29). Not only are they themselves successful and independent as Triple Diamonds, but they have helped many others, regardless of race, faith, age, or origins, to follow in their footsteps. Brought up in an inner city area where many parents had problems with their children and other family relationships, George was especially grateful to Amway for what it meant in improving family life. "This business brings families closer," he said when his own children were still quite young. "And I've noticed great changes in the children—they believe in themselves because they are surrounded by positive attitudes at home."

Jim and Sharon Janz

In the early 1960s, Jim Janz, then a teacher in a small town near Vancouver, British Columbia, became more and more disheartened as he realized that, while teaching was a fine public service, the income was so meager that it stifled all efforts for him and his wife, Sharon, to raise their own children properly. They already had one infant, and Sharon was expecting their second child. By 1964, they were in desperation. "I had to do something," he recalls. "We were borrowing just to stay alive. We lived in a tiny basement apartment, and tried to make do with secondhand furniture and a car that was always breaking down." The break came when the Janzes realized that several of their friends had solved their financial problems by becoming Amway distributors, and they decided to follow suit. Not only did they have equal success, but they discovered that Amway was not simply a medium for making money, but the door to a much more enhanced way of life. Now on the top rung of success as Crown Ambassadors, they are particularly delighted to see that Amway is not just for the older generation. "We see young people joining in droves," says Jim, because this business is just perfect for the nineties. Young people know they have to make their own security, and here is where they can do it."

Dexter and Birdie Yager

Dexter Yager grew up in Rome, New York, where the winters could be cold and bleak and the job opportunities rare for an ambitious young man. Moreover, as he said, "I used to dream of living in a warm climate, owning my own business, and marrying the prettiest girl in the world." While Amway could not help him much with the last-mentioned dream, it certainly made it possible for him to realize the first two. He found the girl first and then, in 1964, got involved in Amway. He might never have fully consummated the relationship had it not been for a thoughtless boss. When Dexter and his wife, having been in Amway less than three months, qualified for a sales trip to Ada, Michigan, the boss refused to give him the time off. After considering his options, Dexter decided to quit the salaried job and strike off completely on his own. Birdie supported him in this resolve—and their lives changed dramatically thereafter. Not only did they become fully active in the business, but over the years they attracted their seven children to Amway as well. "It's marvelous," said Birdie, "the way this business allows children to work at home with their parents, to learn the work ethic from someone who loves them." That was in 1986, and, later that year, Dexter suffered a stroke that left him partially paralyzed and unable to walk. While struggling to regain his ability to walk and function as he once did, Dexter and his family, as a unit, was able to sustain the business at its same peak of success. Needless to say, the business has prospered well over the years (see pages 92–94) and the Yagers along with the Joe Victors, the Stan Evanses, the Frank Delisles, and other old-timers, unmentioned here in these pages but never forgotten, serve as some of the greatest examples of family teamwork in Amway history.

Larry and Linda Riley

Repeatedly, while climbing the corporate ladder, Larry and Linda Riley were forced to pull up stakes and relocate to a new job in a different part of the country. Their story begins in Detroit, where they grew up within ten miles of each other. Yet, they came from different worlds. "I was the youngest of three daughters and very spoiled." Linda laughs. Larry, on the other hand, was born to a teenage mother in the inner city. At ten, he took his first job as a newspaper carrier to help support himself. One summer, while both were home from their respective universities, their paths crossed. Following graduation and Larry's tour of duty in Vietnam, the two married. Larry's degree in business and Linda's degree in home economics landed them jobs with the same appliance manufacturer. They relocated several times as a result of Larry's promotions, before finally being transferred to Washington, D.C. "We had a beautiful home one mile from Lake Michigan," Linda recalls, "but when we relocated to D.C., we could not even afford a house!" But the move proved to be a blessing in disguise. It was in the nation's capital that they began their Amway business, reaching Emerald in relatively short order. "Our professional skills, work habits, and discipline allowed us to grow quickly," Larry observes. "But then, in order to move on, we needed to make some personal changes." The catalyst that jump-started their business was a national award Larry received from his company in 1990, followed by yet another move. "I assumed I was going to get promoted," he recollects. "Instead, they closed my office!" However, his record with the company allowed him to transfer to Atlanta. Linda cried when she heard they were being relocated again. Today, she points out, "It was absolutely the best thing that could have happened. Our son had graduated from high school and was in the Air Force Academy, so it was just the two of us facing our 'empty nest' years. It was the perfect time to ask ourselves what we wanted to do with the rest of our lives." What they chose to do, first, was to fulfill their responsibility to their distributor group already established in Atlanta. "We did not have the right to steal their dream," Linda states. "They didn't know how discouraged we were feeling. But as it always happens when you take your eyes off of yourself and focus on helping others achieve their dreams, the magic of the Amway plan unfolded." As Larry and Linda busily helped their Altanta distributors establish their businesses, their own dreams of achieving Diamond were rekindled. In no time, the Rileys became fired up by the very people they had hoped to inspire. With their help, they took what seemed like an undesirable move and turned it into a long-awaited, hard-earned journey from Emerald to Diamond.

Challenges, Choices, and Change in the 1990s

Needless to say, the batons in many Amway families—including those of the founders—have been handed on successfully to the second generation and even the third. Some say that *sustaining* success may be even more challenging than establishing success during the earlier years of maturation. Be that as it may, the history of the nineties has proved to be exciting, and in some cases dramatic in the overview, looking back. In point of fact, this decade demonstrates the strength of the building process, taking one vital step after another with patience and persistence. In 1990, looking toward the beginning of its fourth decade, Amway opened its doors in Mexico, thus making its coverage of North America almost 100 percent.

A significant event occurred in 1993 when Dick DeVos assumed his role as president of Amway Corporation, thus placing top management in the hands of the second generation of the founders. As he says in his book, *Rediscov-*

ering American Values, "I took the reins and proceeded on
the principal conviction that the key to productivity and
future growth was the unleashing of the creativity, talents,
and energies of Amway people—both employees and distributors—not just the centralized and single-minded pursuit of efficiency. I took the view that profits were not our
immediate goal but would be the natural and appropriate
outcome of doing everything else right. To reinforce our
sense of partnership, we encouraged employees and distributors to work cooperatively and to be truly accountable for
their particular part of the operation."

DeVos also set his sights on making Amway a truly
global company—a very realistic goal in light of the fact
that the company had already established markets in many
countries. This objective necessitated innovative programs
to test not only products, but "visions and values" in new
foreign environments. As DeVos explained, too, Amway
distributors had long been active in international affairs in
acts of public service, apart from their business involve-
ments. "I know Amway distributors," he said, "who took
part in pulling down the Berlin Wall, helped to oust a cor-
rupt dictator in Panama, and came to the rescue of Florida
residents in the wake of Hurricane Hugo. Just as the telecommunications revolution was creating an information
highway accessible to anyone, Amway was creating a
global, human highway that promotes entrepreneurship,
free enterprise, and what my father calls Compassionate
Capitalism."

By 1998, David Van Andel, the son of Jay Van Andel
and now in management as the senior vice president, was
able to report over the Internet, "We're now a global company operating in more than 80 countries and territories. . . . Amway is proud to export its American-style business opportunity to people around the world, but we're also

proud of being a business that was 'Made in America.' ''

In February 1994, an historic agreement was signed by
Billy Florence, president of the Amway Distributors Association U.S. Board; Mark Crawford, a member of the
Amway Distributors Canadian Board; and Tom Eggleston,
then Amway's chief operating officer. The significance of
this event was that it gave distributors in North America an
ongoing voice in decisions that affect their business. It was
cited as ''a step forward that strengthens the partnership
between Amway distributors and the corporation.''

''There are three generations of my family in the business,'' said Jody Victor, chairman of the Amway Distributors Association Council Executive Committee on that
occasion. His family reference was to Joe and Heleyn Victor, who had joined Amway almost at the beginning and
played an important role in its structure and growth during
almost four decades. ''It's very important to us that we
maintain the integrity of the Amway Sales and Marketing
Plan and the vision and faith of the handful of people who
got together in 1959 and began this great idea. My parents
were among that group. With the recent signing of the
Council agreement, we know that faith is concrete and that
trust is bonded even stronger.''

The Amway Distributors Association Board was established as a body of thirty distributors. Fifteen of these individuals were elected by the ADA voting members and
the remaining fifteen chosen by the elected directors of the
council from a slate of distributors nominated by the Amway Corporation to achieve a balanced geographic, pin-
level, and line-of-sponsorship representation. The mission
of the Council was to advise and consult with Amway on
all facets of the business and to take an active role in molding Amway's future.

Some of the council's objectives were long-range and

concerned top-level policy matters, such as the uniformity of operational procedures around the globe as Amway ventured into foreign countries where direct-selling concepts are little known. Others were more specific and directed at expediting improvements in relationships and communications. One example in the mid-1990s was the preparation and release of a Spanish-language edition of the Amway Business Kit, to provide Spanish-speaking distributors in North America with more effective methods of starting new businesses. The U.S./Spanish Kit featured all of the concepts and components of the previously released English version, and thus was complete unto itself.

The council also had a hand in the conceptualization and implementation of the North American Growth Program. This program, announced by Doug DeVos, who had recently been elected senior vice president/managing director of Amway North America, was introduced in 1997 to provide to qualifiers "an amazing array of rewards, not only for this fiscal year but up through the year 2000."

By that time, the emergence of the second generation in the Amway administration was an accomplished fact, especially following the selection of Steve Van Andel as the company's new chairman in 1995. Together with President Dick DeVos, he had formed what they called the Office of the Chief Executive. They viewed this relationship as one that was vital in keynoting Amway's ever-present spirit of *cooperation*, which assures the durability of the free-enterprise system.

Dedication of an Innovative and Informative Visitor Center

In December 1997, after months of anticipation, Amway unveiled the new crown jewel of its World Headquarters in

Ada, Michigan, when the Amway Visitor Center was dedicated to Amway cofounders Rich DeVos and Jay Van Andel. In the opening ceremony, Amway Chairman Steve Van Andel and President Dick DeVos offered the visitor center as a tribute to the vision and dream shared by their fathers. Bernice Hansen, one of Amway's first distributors, and Bob Rooker, one of its first employees, joined Van Andel and DeVos in reminiscing about the early days and marveling over the cofounders' lifelong achievements. It is these memories that are brought to life through archival photographs, interactive audiovisual presentations, and mementos collected over the years. One feature is a self-guided journey through the "Amway story," which began nearly two decades before the company actually was formed in 1959.

Innovative screen computer technology lets guests take a visit to Amway's affiliates around the world. Hands-on kiosks answer frequently asked questions about the Amway opportunity and take visitors, step-by-step, through the life cycle of a product. The many ways Amway and distributors worldwide are involved in their communities are showcased through giant photographs and touch-screen technology. Since no one else could possibly tell the Amway story as effectively as Rich DeVos and Jay Van Andel, or explain the philosophies and values behind this unique success story, the exhibit also features a video collage of excerpts from recorded speeches of DeVos and Van Andel, making it possible for guests to hear the story as told by the founders themselves.

The centerpiece of the visitor center is a sixty-five-seat multimedia theater. Guests begin their visitor center tour in this state-of-the-art studio with a showing of *A World of Opportunity,* an audiovisual presentation that sets the stage for the guest to experience the rest of the center to its fullest.

The visitor center was designed by a team led by Jonathan Horn of Derse Exhibits. With locations around the country, Derse Exhibits has been designing, building, and managing integrated custom exhibit programs since 1948 for a number of clients, including Nintendo, Hormel, American Airlines, and Ameritech.

Public Service: An Amway Heritage

Several years ago Amway distributors John and Melodee Williams of Washington offered to help a landscaper friend with a volunteer project. But the project has truly blossomed over what it started out to be. That's because John and Melodee have been joined by more than twenty-five others from their distributor organization who spend an entire day twice each year planting several thousand flower bulbs at a local facility for people in need.

"Every October," says Melodee, "we plant loads of crocuses, daffodils, tulips, hyacinths, and winter-flowering pansies. In May we pull all of those and replant with dahlias, lilies, and many colorful annuals." The bulbs are donated by a large international bulb distributor in their area.

"The biannual planting has become a highlight of the season for all of us and our kids," she explains, adding that the house is a home-away-from-home for families of children who are being treated for cancer at nearby Children's Hospital. "We get a chance to visit with some of the families staying there, including some of the children who are sick. It is truly a life-enriching experience for all of us."

Far from this colorful scene, another Amway distributor project has been blooming in a different fashion during the 1990s. To Norm Stout of Ohio, the project seemed relatively straightforward: Go into a Mexican village and rebuild a church that had been destroyed by a hurricane.

Norm and twelve others flew into Puerto Escondido, Oaxaca, in February of 1998, where they were shocked to see that the devastation was much worse than they had expected. "All crops had been destroyed," he said, "along with many homes and buildings. The local people had nothing. And we had no equipment. Villagers had carried in six thousand pounds of cement on their backs, or on burros, to try to start rebuilding."

Norm and his volunteer crew mixed cement on the ground with shovels and hauled it in five-gallon buckets. They made cement blocks in makeshift forms right there on the site. Although it seemed almost impossible in retrospect, the Amway team had built, within seven days, a small concrete church to replace the mud-and-stick structure that had been blown away. During that week, filled with so many unforeseen happenings, Norm stumbled on yet another unexpected circumstance. "I discovered," he said with a radiant smile, "that two of the Mexican nationals we'd brought with us were distributors of Amway products, as was a Guatemalan missionary."

On a much broader scale in the area of good works, many independent distributors and employees in the United States and Canada volunteer their time and talent to support Junior Achievement and its mission to inspire and educate young people to value free enterprise, understand business and economics, and develop entrepreneurial and leadership skills. Junior Achievement is the world's largest and fastest-growing nonprofit economic education organization, each year reaching more than 2.6 million American students in cities, suburbs, and rural areas alike. Amway volunteers teach the Junior Achievement curriculum to students in kindergarten through high school and advise older students in the Junior Achievement Project Business evening programs.

In addition, Amway, together with *Newsweek* magazine, is active in sponsoring an awareness campaign that promotes economic literacy among youth through the Junior Achievement program. They have also undertaken a national survey, "Redefining the American Dream," which is reported on the Junior Achievement website. These efforts have promoted workforce readiness for American students and provided parents with helpful ideas on how they can instill in their children a balanced view on money and spending. Through advertisements, they have recognized outstanding students and the role Junior Achievement has played in helping them realize their potential.

Although Amway participaties in philanthropic giving— through its distributors and the corporation alike—in ways too numerous to mention here, one project stands out as a shining example. It is known nationwide as Amway & Easter Seals: The Courage to Dream, the Opportunity to Succeed.

The mission of Easter Seals is to help people achieve greater independence and to provide programs and services that help people with disabilities live with equality, dignity, and independence. In the United States, the District of Columbia, and Puerto Rico, more than one million people are served through a network of Easter Seal affiliate societies. Easter Seals Canada serves children up to age eighteen by way of ten provincial offices.

Over the years, independent distributors have helped raise millions of dollars for Easter Seals to help people with disabilities achieve greater independence. In fact, since 1983, Amway Corporation and distributors in the United States and Canada have raised more than $23 million for this worthy cause.

Money is raised in a variety of ways, providing an excellent opportunity for distributors to work together for a common, worthwhile cause and to have fun at the same time. Fund-raising events include car washes, bowl-a-thons, golf tournaments, bake sales, and fashion shows. Distributors participate in these "fun"-raising events throughout the year, and have raised close to $2 million for each year of the late 1990s.

The Benefits of Collaboration

During the 1990s Amway was successful in working with major manufacturers to bring to the direct-selling market products of very high quality and international reputation. This was particularly significant as Amway moved more and more into other countries around the world where this kind of prestige was important.

In the spring of 1997, for example, Amway and Waterford Crystal, Ltd., announced an exclusive affiliation for a new line of fine-quality crystal giftware. And thus the Amway Diamond Collection by Marquis became the newest addition to the extensive line of products for the end of the 1990s. The hallmark of this collection is an exclusive diamond-cut design created by Waterford, defined as "one of the ten most respected brands in the United States," and brought to life by the great crystal makers of Europe. The first product under this new affiliation was an eight-inch vase, available for purchase only through independent distributors. It was designed by Michael Fanning, a leading member of the Waterford design team who is known for his innovative design concepts. He has created the Ballylee, Kilrane, and Wicklow patterns for Waterford and the Festival, Canterbury, and Windflower designs for Marquis by Waterford Crystal.

The affiliation with Waterford was designed to provide distributors with a prestigious, exclusive line of products to market worldwide. "Waterford has a history of excellence in the crystal and glassware field just as Amway has a tradition of excellence in the direct-selling industry," said David Brenner, senior vice president of Market Development.

This impressive affiliation in no way diminished Amway's goals to market those products that had historically been Amway's "bread and butter" for four decades. For anyone who thought otherwise, the Marketing Department came up with a dazzling statistic about one of its oldest and most popular products: *"Throughout the world, distributors sold enough L.O.C. Multi-Purpose Cleaner in one year to scrub a kitchen floor the size of Utah's Great Salt Lake!"*

CHAPTER EIGHT

Foreign Expansion

The distinguished British novelist of the nineteenth century, William Makepeace Thackeray, once wrote that the world was a looking glass that gave back to all persons the reflection of their own faces. People had the power to interpret the world in their own image, no matter where they happened to live. The history of Amway has proven the truth of Thackeray's perception, demonstrating again and again that individuals can control their destinies to a great extent by their attitudes and outlooks, as well as by their actions. What works in Keokuk, Iowa; Friendship, Maine; and Love, Texas can also work in Fromantle, Australia, Kawasaki, Japan; and Llanfairfechan, Wales. It requires considerable imagination to picture the walls of the Van Andel and DeVos basements that defined the world of Amway less than three decades ago and see this cramped space magically expanding into facilities serving some forty countries and territories. Yet it does not stretch credulity quite so much to picture circles of people reaching out to more and more circles of people until eventually their le-

*gions encompass the globe. The people-to-people image, by
contrast to the image of physical expansion, is more like
an arithmetical progression. Yet the numbers are secondary
to the philosophy and concept that nurtured the growth and
made it possible. "The entrepreneurial spirit seems to be
in everybody, everywhere," says Rich DeVos when trying
to explain how it was possible for Amway International to
establish 11 foreign affiliates in as many years.*

"What Amway does is provide the opportunity."

—Wilbur Cross and Gordon Olson,
Commitment to Excellence, *1986*

WHAT SEEMED LIKE a miracle of international expansion
back in the mid-1980s was but a prelude of things to come.
Before the end of the 1990s, the expansion would not only
double, but be immeasurably strengthened by the caliber,
expertise, and proficiency of the distributorships abroad.

The history of Amway's global development is one
whose framework was based, from the beginning, on commitment, unflagging dedication, insight, and just plain hard
work. The overseas potential first became apparent when,
in 1965, Jay Van Andel was invited to be one of seventy
trade delegates to explore opportunities abroad. The purpose of the delegation, formed by then Michigan Governor
George Romney, was to establish trade contacts between
Michigan and Western Europe. Although Van Andel became convinced that foreign soil was fertile ground, he and
his partner decided to defer overseas expansion in favor of
devoting full time to their vigorous North American operations. They failed to reckon with eager distributors who
also realized the potential on the other side of the Atlantic.

After Amway of Canada had been established in 1962
as an extension of the company's domestic operations, it

had quickly and effectively proved that the philosophy and
the Sales and Marketing Plan could be successfully "exported." In a sense, though Canada was not considered
"foreign" in the strictest sense of the word, Amway did
have to face the problems of crossing an international border and dealing with another language in those regions
where French was the primary tongue. Also, opening the
business in Puerto Rico brought the language problems into
the picture, as well as the difficulties of making shipments
overseas.

Getting wind of the fact that management was at least
exploring the idea of global operations, distributors began
deluging headquarters with requests for overseas sponsoring information.

Prompted by the brimming interest and the sheer numbers of the would-be foreign entrepreneurs, DeVos and Van
Andel began to survey and study possible international
markets. By 1969, they had fixed their sights firmly on
Australia. Although the choice was termed "unscientific"
and made without intensive market research, Australia was
selected for its cultural and economic similarity to the
United States. A more telling reason, supported by the Marketing Division, was that the Amway Sales and Marketing
Plan and the concept of person-to-person selling would
"prove irresistible to the enterprising Australians."

"We like the spirit of the people," DeVos explained at
the time. "They are looking for opportunities; they have
real faith in their country and in themselves, and they believe in the future. They're gung ho, and Amway's going
to give them the opportunity to make it."

The Amway advance team spent almost a year laying
the groundwork for the new operation before going to Syd-
ney, Australia, to devote some ten months expediting plans
for the new foreign operation. Amway quickly discovered

that establishing a business in a foreign country was extremely complex, requiring close collaboration with attorneys to make sure plans conformed to Australian laws, developing an appropriate product line, lining up distributors, providing detailed orientation and training, designing new literature, and recruiting an Australian to manage the new company.

Soon after it opened in April 1971, the new operation began attracting attention in the American, as well as the Australian, press. *Business Abroad* magazine reported in its July issue that Amway's ''entrepreneurial gospel has been spreading like wildfire among Australian housewives and their husbands. Five nights a week groups of 150 to 250 cheering and clapping Australians have been assembling to listen to the message Amway Corporation has just exported from the U.S.: how to make a better-than-average living through sales.''

An Anecdotal Lesson from Australia

One of the Diamond Direct Distributors in Australia, Peter Javelin, made an interesting observation when he pointed out that the national symbol, the kangaroo, doesn't jump backward. Rather, it often stays still, and looks around and surveys other perspectives.

''My wife and I learned from the school of hard knocks before we started in Amway,'' said Javelin. ''We had a paint factory, a business we fell into and couldn't seem to get out of. Finally we sold it and got into electrical appliances, gas installations—and you name it. We started sales teams and we made money and we invested in various stocks because we heard you had to speculate to accumulate. We believed it, but we ended up broke.

''Well, like the kangaroo, to start moving forward

you've got to take the big jump. And that's what we did, into Amway. And we're very excited about what we've seen and heard about what's happening in Australia and around the world of Amway. It's excitement. It's enthusiasm. It's motivation for the dream that can come true.''

A Fast Start—Then an Impasse

Although Amway signed up about four hundred distributors during the first month of operation and soon afterward was reporting the first Direct Distributors, the Australian business did not take off as expected. Worse yet, it slowed down and did not seem ready to budge.

Investigation showed that the problem was not with the Amway concept itself or the mode of operation. It lay with the product line. Amway had contracted with Australian vendors to manufacture all products to its exacting specifications. But quality control proved to be a major weakness, along with erratic production and supply. Although the outlook was anything but optimistic, the experience proved to be very beneficial in the long run. It was finally determined that the production and shipping departments in Ada, Michigan, could supply Australia with products more cheaply and reliably than if they were made Down Under. This practice kept the business in Amway's own plants where there was a profit-making potential, created local employment, improved the national balance of trade, and maximized quality control.

Most importantly, the Australian experience, unlucky though it may have seemed at the time, established the precedent whereby most overseas markets are supplied today by American-made products that are then exported to the foreign distribution centers.

The ultimate success of what Amway's marketing peo-

ple referred to as "the Australian Experiment" encouraged
Amway to launch a string of overseas affiliates in Western
European countries where free enterprise permitted the
proper functioning of the Sales and Marketing Plan. As had
been the case with Australia, these European markets were
selected on the basis of each country's economic and cultural compatibility with the United States. Over a period of
seven years, European affiliates were established as wholly
owned, independent enterprises in six countries: the United
Kingdom and the Republic of Ireland in 1973, West Germany in 1975, France in 1977, the Netherlands in 1978,
and Belgium and Switzerland in 1980.

With an eye on Asia, Amway selected Hong Kong for
the first affiliate in the Far East, in part because many of
its citizens were already familiar with American marketing
methods, products, and policies. As in the case of Australia,
sales got off to a slow start in the mid-1970s, but then
began to increase steadily and, in some cases, dramatically.
The steady growth of the business motivated Amway, in
1976, to add Malaysia to its growing foreign affiliations,
and this market became one of the most successful in Asia,
based on per capita income and population. One year after
it was started, the affiliate experienced the fastest growth
rate of any overseas operation up until that time, and within
three more years was quadrupling its annual sales figure.
Equal success was experienced when Amway Taiwan was
established in 1982.

The Enigma of Japan

Despite the success in the Far East, the question arose
on numerous occasions: What about Japan? Would Japanese women, for instance, have enough social freedom to
become distributors? And, even if they did, would Western

products be suitable for Japanese tastes and needs? Amway had already proved that language and cultural differences were not insurmountable barriers *if* there were the necessary elements of motivation and the desire to become financially independent.

The decision was made to proceed, and in 1979 Japan became Amway's fourth Asian affiliate. Although economically developed and long engaged in trade with the United States, Japan presents more cultural differences than perhaps any other society in which Amway does business.

The business flourished so well that Japan rivals the United States as Amway's largest market. In 1997 Dick DeVos said, "While many of America's leading manufacturers proclaimed that Japanese markets were closed to U.S. companies, Japan was embracing the spirit of our way of doing business. Now, in fact, Amway sales in Japan are approaching two billion dollars annually, ranking us as one of the top-performing foreign companies in Japan."

The Emergence of Women on the Asian Business Scene

According to John Naisbitt, an economist with a strong knowledge of foreign affairs, there has been a considerable revolution in Asia in the business world during the last two decades in the matter of the acceptance of women in the workplace. He gives a number of examples, including the fact that the number of female managers in Singapore has nearly tripled in the last decade, 20 percent of the managerial positions in Hong Kong are held by women, some 80 percent of new businesses in Japan are being originated by women, and about 25 percent of all those started in China. Evidence shows that Amway has been a substantial factor in this shift of male/female balance overseas, since it treats the sexes equally in all business matters, and has made it possible for many Asian women to start their own businesses—something that would have been almost impossible two decades ago. Add to this the fact that many of Amway's products—especially those for household use and personal care—are female-oriented, and thus readily promoted by female distributors.

Global Challengers

As its foreign operations spread, Amway was discovering that distributors abroad were faced with many other challenges besides the initial one of overseas delivery and quality control. Here are a few of the problems, for example, that had to be solved:

- Coping with unfamiliar and complex customs regulations, and sometimes dealing with irrational or poorly informed customs officials.

- Storing and marketing products in tropical regions where the humidity was excessive and temperatures often exceeded 120° F.

- Keeping foodstuffs fresh in storage areas where the air-conditioning was nonexistent, or unreliable at best.

- Protecting perishable products from swarms of insects, rodents, and other predators.

- Providing containers and packaging that would withstand severe vibrations and impact while being transported along rock-strewn roads or in the clutches of makeshift or defective handling equipment.

- Varying the packaging to conform to unique sizing, labeling, and weight specifications.

- Making sure that user instructions, guarantees, and any legal warnings were perfectly accurate in the language of the countries where the products were being marketed.

Amway was faced, too, with an enormous language challenge, not only abroad but in North America where distributors and shippers were often dealing with distributors, customers, and services on other continents. Today, for example, distributors in North America can now place orders and get answers to business questions in any of eighty-five different languages.

Venturing into China

There seemed to be no end to the countries whose citizens were eager to try products that exemplified the American way of life. Three new affiliates sprouted in 1994, in the Czech Republic, Turkey, and Slovakia. The year 1995 was particularly active, with the arrival of six more, in El Salvador, Honduras, Chile, Slovenia, Uruguay, and China.

China was a big surprise to many people, even within Amway, since it had long had the reputation as being inhospitable to American firms. Of this venture, Dick DeVos said, "The same government that sent soldiers into Tiananmen Square has welcomed the manufacture and sale of Amway products in mainland China, taking what I hope is an important step toward freedom and opportunity in that country."

It is interesting that China, Japan, and other Asian nations are represented in the two major affiliates that have gone public: Amway Japan, Ltd., and Amway Asia Pacific, Ltd., both listed on the New York Stock Exchange. The latter is the exclusive distribution vehicle for the Amway Corporation in Australia, Brunei, the People's Republic of China, Hong Kong, Macau, Malaysia, New Zealand, Taiwan, and Thailand. With annual sales close to $900 million, and a core distributor force of some 670,000 distributors, Amway Asia Pacific is one of the largest direct-selling companies in the region.

In its annual report for 1997, Amway Asia Pacific reported that it had opened in ten new provinces in China that year, including the direct municipalities of Beijing, Chongqing, and Tianjian, and thus had the potential to serve a market of more than 300 million people in fourteen provinces. The China market was called "the backbone of Amway Asia Pacific."

"Although economists may differ on the precise numbers," reported Chairman Steve Van Andel and President Dick DeVos, "China is clearly one of the largest economies in the world, and with a population of an estimated 1.2 billion people, it offers us more potential customers than all our other markets combined." The China venture started with five household cleaners, but within two years had grown to more than thirty household and personal care products. Amway's presence in China also included a manufacturing plant in Guangzhou and plans for another plant in Shanghai, to produce nutrition and skin care products.

The new venture in China proceeded surprisingly well—until the spring of 1998. On April 22, Amway released this statement: "The government of China issued today a new directive affecting the entire direct selling industry. The directive requires immediate cessation of direct selling activities, and requires that all direct selling companies modify their mode of operations. Amway Corporation understands and respects the Chinese government's decision to take these additional steps to protect consumers from illegal pyramid scams, which have become a more serious social problem in recent months. We recognize these steps are aimed at stopping illegal activities, but they also affect the entire direct selling industry, including legitimate companies like Amway.''

Amway China then prepared to take steps that would maintain its commitment to its distributors, while at the same time working within unique Chinese regulations. The steps to be taken were specific to China, said Amway, with no plans to extend these steps to other countries. ''Given the Chinese government's directive to all direct sellers to modify their mode of operations, we are now working to modify our distribution system. Our final plan will build on several strengths that already exist in the Amway business, including our 40 product service centers nationwide. These facilities are centrally located in population centers in some 14 provinces and four direct municipalities. They are managed and staffed by Amway China professionals with a strong commitment to outstanding customer service.

''What has not changed is Amway's strong commitment to China and to independent distributors, trainers, customers and employees. AAP has invested nearly $100 million in China over the last five years, and we continue to believe in the long-term business opportunities of this enormous and rapidly growing market.''

On June 22, 1998, the Chinese government issued a new directive and provided guidelines whereby previously approved direct selling companies could modify their operations and resume business in China. Amway Asia Pacific was greatly encouraged that this new directive provided Amway China with the legal basis for the continued use of independent sales representatives, which was a fundamental of the business, and which had been the focus of the company's discussions with the Chinese government for the previous two months.

On July 20, Amway Asia Pacific announced that Amway China would resume business operations the next day, having received approval for its revised plan from the Chinese national government. "We are pleased to receive this formal notice of approval, which is a major step forward for the company," said Steve Van Andel, speaking as Chairman of Amway Asia Pacific. "It responds to the unique situation which exists in China, while at the same time allows us to achieve long-term growth in partnership with our team of independent salespeople. We are pleased to see that Amway's tradition of providing an opportunity for individuals to derive income proportionate to their efforts and ability can be preserved in China as it is around the world."

Amway not only managed to avert what might have been a serious setback in global relationships and operations, but was the first company so approved for business resumption by the Chinese government during this sensitive period of transition.

Reaching Out

In other parts of the globe, Amway had already continued its steady march by the time the China operation was back in swing. In April 1997, Amway Philippines officially opened its doors for business at its headquarters in Makati and product selection centers in Quezon City, Las Pinas, and Cebu. This was a period when the country was experiencing strong economic growth and where there had been considerable interest in the eleven types of home care and personal care products that were to be introduced initially.

This new venture also provided jobs for more than sixty people, as well as producing income for the entrepreneurs who saw their opportunity as distributors.

One of the most important links in the Amway global chain was to be the company's entry into the African continent with a new South Africa affiliate. On September 22, 1997, Amway announced that, after expanding into Australia and most of Europe, Asia, and South America, it had opened for business on a sixth continent, with an affiliate in South Africa. Amway South Africa, with headquarters in Cape Town, thus became the forty-fourth country where Amway had affiliate operations, among the most recent having been those in Costa Rica, Greece, and Colombia.

Referring to the new African operation, President Dick DeVos said market openings were most significant for the opportunity they offered to more people worldwide. "Over the past decade," he said, "social and political changes around the world have improved conditions for small businesses and direct selling. Where conditions are appropriate, we have continued to introduce the Amway opportunity in new markets and given thousands of people the vehicle to own their own business." This was to prove especially appropriate, as well as innovative, on a continent that had seldom been hospitable to entrepreneurs and others who wanted personal independence.

About the time that the company was celebrating its entry onto a new continent, Amway's management was wrestling with another problem on the international front—one whose outcome could be critical. Serious legal questions had been raised in Belgium about Amway's method of doing business. It was the old protestation all over again by detractors who inferred that Amway was conducting a "pyramid" scheme. But in late 1997, in a decision that would lead to further acceptance and growth of direct selling in Europe, the Brussels Commercial Court confirmed that Amway and its multilevel method of direct selling complied fully with Belgian law. The court rejected assertions by the Belgian State's Ministry of Economic Affairs that Amway had infringed Article 84 of the country's law on Unfair Trade Practices, which deals with pyramid sales and chain selling. In distinguishing between legitimate multilevel direct sales companies, such as Amway, and unethical chain sellers prohibited under Article 84, the court stated: "It is neither the intention of Amway, nor of its distributors, to merely recruit new distributors. As in traditional retailing, all the profits result from the sale of products to customers."

The court further ruled that "Amway's multilevel sales system has different levels because of the difference in compensation to each distributor, based on his/her sales volume. Distributors purchase products directly from Amway, rather than from other distributors. Thus, distributors assume the same footing toward the customer and toward each other."

The court also considered the diversity of consumer protection measures provided by Amway in its sales system, noting the provisions to be "more than effective to ensure that neither the product sellers nor their customers can be harmed; that Amway seems to be able to observe its own rules and not to make promises that it could not keep."

Specifically, the judge enumerated the following consumer protection measures: that the company required no large up-front investments, that all distributor investments were protected by return guarantees, that distributors were protected from the risk of overstocking, and that customers were protected with solid guarantees for product returns and refunds.

Amway Belgium spokesperson Michel Goossens said,

"For the 5,600 people in Belgium who own their own businesses selling quality Amway products, the court's decision underscores the valuable role that legitimate multilevel marketing companies can play in today's changing and challenging economy."

Another of the seemingly endless strings of claims against the company served to reinforce the fact that its policies and operations were not only legitimate and sound, but that they were applicable in good faith anywhere in the world.

To close out the year, the Amway global march continued with the establishment of an affiliate in Romania in November. This was particularly notable because free-enterprise opportunities had been unavailable to Romania's twenty-three million citizens for many years.

Amway was also honored that year for its efforts around Planet Earth and recognized "for extraordinary conservation efforts and achievements" on behalf of the ecology. Dave Van Andel, senior vice president/managing director—America and Europe, accepted a Green Globe Award from the Rain Forest Alliance on behalf of the company and its distributors and employees worldwide for more than fifty environmental sponsorships underway in twenty-three countries. This honor was blessed by many others during this period in the company's history, including recognition by the United Nations Environment Programme.

Recognition came in another, more subtle, form when it was realized abroad that Amway was becoming a real boon to the local business community wherever it started in business. Each Amway foreign affiliate functions as a commercial entity within its market, significantly contributing to the economic development and regional quality of life. For example, each affiliate provides:

- Employment for local staff members and employees
- Training and orientation for both groups
- Income opportunities for a large population base
- Contributions to the tax base, including income taxes
- The payment of substantial import duties and excise taxes
- Highest-quality products and services for local citizens
- Hiring of local services, such as printing and shipping
- Leasing of facilities, such as warehouses and offices
- Purchases of local equipment and supplies
- Use of local transportation facilities
- Experience and business training for citizens
- Help in drafting effective direct-selling legislation
- Contributions to educational and humanitarian causes
- Sharing technological know-how and experience

Shock Waves Around the World

The year 1998 opened auspiciously on the international front in the matter of new foreign businesses, starting with a new affiliate in the Dominican Republic in mid-January in support of some twenty-five hundred entrepreneurs. Dominicans had actually been familiar with Amway products for more than twenty years, but had not had the easy access afforded to them by the new affiliate and an Amway Service Center in Santo Domingo.

Another highlight was the opening of a new affiliate in India, the world's second most-populated nation, in May. This was a huge operation in that more than 100,000 new distributors have embraced the business opportunity in that country since it opened in the spring.

But there were distant rumblings of trouble on the horizon. Amway management was not blind to the problem. In its 1997 annual report for Amway Asia Pacific, for example, a passage entitled "Initiatives for Growth" had this to say: "The Malaysia-Thailand region, historically our most profitable region, reported record operating income in fiscal 1997. However, in the fourth quarter we saw a number of challenges. Currency devaluation in Malaysia and Thailand and the resulting economic turmoil adversely affected sales and sponsoring in the fourth quarter of fiscal 1997, a trend which we expect will continue into fiscal 1998."

Similar premonitions of economic trouble were echoed in the annual report for Amway Japan, where 1997 was described as "a year of both triumphs and disappointment."

Currency devaluations, not only in Asia but in other regions of the world, tended to reduce margins, since the majority of the goods sold were being purchased from Amway Corporation with U.S. dollars.

On October 26, 1998, Amway announced global estimated retail sales of $5.7 billion for the fiscal year ended August 31, 1998. Impressive though this figure seemed in comparison with previous annual reports during the company's forty-year history, it was acknowledged to be *a decline of more than 18 percent* from estimated retail sales the previous year. This figure represented the combined results at estimated retail for the forty-nine affiliate markets supported by privately owned Amway Corporation and its publicly traded sister companies, Amway Asia Pacific, Ltd., and Amway Japan, Ltd., which had announced their annual sales separately during the previous ten days.

"Fiscal 1998 was a challenging year," stated Amway Chairman Steve Van Andel. "Nearly half of our business is in Asian markets where economic upheaval resulted in weak consumer demand. Our revenues were further reduced when translated from weak Asian currencies back into strong U.S. dollars."

About 85 percent of the decline Amway experienced during the 1998 fiscal year was attributed to factors associated with the strong U.S. dollar and the weak Asian economy. In fact, the majority of Amway's decline in sales could be attributed to just five affiliate markets: Japan, Korea, China, Malaysia, and Thailand, which together declined by almost $1 billion in estimated retail sales. Despite these disappointing results, Amway has enjoyed an 18 percent compound annual growth rate since it began reporting estimated retail sales in 1964.

"We've enjoyed phenomenal growth, including double-digit increases during the early and mid 1990s, said Amway President Dick DeVos. "We remain confident in the fundamentals of the Amway business and we're finding new ways to energize our business through the products and the business opportunity we offer our distributors and customers. Because of what we've accomplished in the face of many challenges, fiscal 1998 remains one of our best years ever."

While the Amway Corporation builds on these and other successes, it was also taking actions to align costs more closely with business volume. Among other ways of realignment, Amway announced in September 1998 a Voluntary Early Retirement Program, offering employees the opportunity to retire early, thus gradually tightening the ranks without having to make severe cuts in the existing roster. Nearly 300 accepted the offer, and about 250 positions were eliminated from Amway's global employee ranks of 12,000 people.

"We remain very optimistic about the future of this company," said Steve Van Andel. "Its foundation is very solid, with excellent products, loyal consumers, and the desire of Amway distributor entrepreneurs around the world to achieve through a business of their own. We believe that the best business opportunity in the world continues to be an Amway business."

CHAPTER NINE

New Generations and Old Legacies

In the lobby of the Amway World Headquarters in Ada, Michigan, hangs a mural that is 7 feet high and 20 feet long. It's called "The Bond." Presented to Jay Van Andel and Rich DeVos in 1985 by artist Paul Collins, the painting weaves together a series of vignettes that tell the Amway story: the hard road to success, the country that made it possible, the legendary distributors who to this day propel Amway to new levels of achievement. All are bonded together—the people, the values, the country, the history—to tell this remarkable story.

What stands out more than anything else in "The Bond" is the role of family in the lives of the cofounders and in the milestones they have achieved. The centerpiece of the mural is a portrait of Jay, flanked on one side by his wife, Betty, and their four children; next to Jay is Rich, flanked on the other side by his wife, Helen, and their four children.

Family stands at the center of the Amway miracle—not just for the founders but for Amway distributors both famous and unknown around the world. Virtually every per-

son I have heard from in this business has praised Amway for the role it has played in strengthening or even saving their families.

It is a business that families can build together and pass on to future generations. It is a business that can be built without putting the family's financial foundation in jeopardy: one spouse can initially take the lead, while the other continues to draw a steady paycheck from a salaried position. It is a business that has prevented divorce and prompted touching reconciliations of parents and children after decades of estrangement. It is a business that serves as a loving family for those who have none.

—*James W. Robinson,* Empire of Freedom

DURING ITS FIRST twenty years of operation, Amway became known as a company whose distibutors were family-oriented and that in many cases inspired children to join the business in an even more tightly knit family group. One of the prime examples, which has often been cited, is that of the Victor family, which earned the distinction of being the first to have three generations in the business. Joe and Heleyne Victor were one of the original Direct Distributors, working with Rich and Jay way back when there was only one product to sell. Their son, Jody, became familiar with the business—because it was held right in the family living room. He went on to college, studied law, and initially had no intention of joining Amway. However, as he began to see what a great life it was for his parents, he too decided to start a new career. He and his wife, Kathy, were successful, and in time their son Steve, and his wife, Marcia, became Direct Distributors, and the third-generation "giant step" was a reality.

It is a signifiant fact that, during the last twenty years,

the Amway Corporation in Ada, Michigan, has followed the same "family" pattern as many of its most successful distributors—by seeing the children, and later the grandchildren, of the founders enter the business. It is important to note here that neither of the founders ever put any pressure on sons and daughters to follow in their footsteps. If anything, they leaned in the opposite direction, and were supportive of any career searches or decisions that were made.

Nan Van Andel was the first of Jay's children to begin working at Amway, where she started out in the Auditing department, before going on to Personnel and then Communications. She started almost immediately after graduating from college. Amway was her second home. "There was never any big decision that had to be made to go into Amway," she recalled. "This is my life. It always has been. I have all that early bonding with the business from childhood. I understood where it all came from and all the things my dad and Rich did to make it grow. So it just never occurred to me to consider another career. Coming to work at Amway was as natural as breathing."

Dick DeVos was the first of Rich's children to take a similar step, cherishing even his childhood days with a father who was deeply committed to this whole new kind of business concept. "Dad took us on some of his business trips," he recalled. "We got to know the Amway people. Although what he was doing was innovative, and different from any other kinds of marketing, he was always confident, always knew what he was achieving. He must have realized that those things build in you a feeling for the business and a real affection for it. By the time I had to decide what I wanted to do with my life, I liked Amway and thought I could make a contribution."

Nan and Dick started at entry-level positions in the Am-

way plant in Ada, Michigan. It was hardly a glamorous
start, as they learned the ropes in every part of the company
in Ada, doing necessary chores and learning how to get
along with other people in many aspects of the business.
After what they described as a "wall-to-wall experience"
in many departments, they became the first members of a
systematic training program to prepare them for eventual
leadership roles.

In 1977, recognizing that there was strong evidence that
the second generation would play an increasing part in the
company's growth, the founders assigned their consultant,
Clair Knox, the project of planning a five-year management
training program designed to familiarize its participants
with all aspects of the company, following the dictum that
knowledge and experience are the best teachers. Its objective was clearly stated: "To have the second generation
qualified to carry on the well established philosophy so
carefully emphasized and practiced by the founders." Under the supervision of senior staff members, the two train-
ees (and later their brothers and sisters) spent time in every
part of the company's operations, from reception room to
boardroom. They also did their stints as distributors in the
field, selling Amway products to customers and recruiting
new prospects for the distributor force.

One important directive was emphasized to them, as well
as to other offspring of the founders who followed: to learn
and understand how essential every single job and every
single person was in the company.

Jay's eldest son, Steve, was not at all certain about his
preferences, and for some time steered away from Amway
and explored other career choices. Like many young men
of his generation, he did not immediately "find himself,"
and was not ready to make any commitment. It took him,
in fact, almost two years of job evaluation and reflection

before he decided to enter the management training program and devote himself to the Amway work ethic. Dave Van Andel is said to have been more Amway-directed than his brother at the start, making an early decision that he wanted to follow in his father's footsteps. The others of the eight Van Andel/DeVos children who are in Amway and now serving on the Policy Board are Cheri DeVos Vander Weide, Doug DeVos, Dan DeVos, and Barb Van Andel Gaby.

"Being the son or daughter of the cofounder of a large company is not easy," wrote Jay Van Andel in his perceptive autobiography, *An Enterprising Life*. "My children have had to deal with pressures and conflicts that I never faced. Growing up working in Amway, they were scrutinized more closely than any of the other employees. In management positions in Amway, my children, and Rich's as well, have had to work twice as hard as anyone else, and often they don't receive the credit due them. If they do well in management and the business grows, people will say, 'Well, they had the business handed to them on a silver platter.' If the business does not do well under their leadership, people will say, 'Look, they destroyed the fine business their fathers built.' The children also had to deal with the incessant questioning and doubting: 'Are they here because of who their father is, or because they're qualified for the job?' Of course, they would most likely not be at Amway if it were not for my presence there. But that takes nothing away from their management abilities. Each of my children, and Rich's children, are very well qualified for the work they do with Amway, as proven by Amway's continued success under their leadership on the Policy Board. With Steve now as chairman and Dick DeVos as president, Amway is in extremely capable hands."

How did the sons and daughters of Rich and Jay feel

about entering the business as close relatives of the founders? "I think we have all been extremely sensitive to the
family connections," said Dick DeVos in an interview with
Amway historian Charles Paul Conn in the mid-1980s,
"and I don't think we've had any problems. You develop
a bit of a sixth sense about when people are using you or
not. Dad and Jay know they have to maintain an arm's
length relationship. They stay out of the way. Both Dad
and Jay do a great job of that."

Nan agreed with this assessment, telling Conn, "Initially
people are concerned about one's last name or one's position. Then they come to know you as a person and relate
to you as the person you are. People around here don't
think much about the family connection. During the training period, I would come into a place to work with people,
and after one or two days, I was just Nan, not the boss's
daughter. Then it is what I am and do that matters."

The illusion of family "connection" is diluted even
more by the fact that Nan, like her peers, has a deep sense
of duty and commitment to Amway and its whole ideology.
"I believe Amway is important," she asserts. "What we
do is important, and we are determined to keep it moving.
I don't know whether corporate competition is that important to me, in the conventional sense. I'd like Amway to
be Number One, and all that, but that's not what really is
important to me—or I think to Dick. What *is* important is
to make sure we are meeting the needs of the distributor
force. We want everybody, from the guy who signed up
yesterday to the one who has been in from the beginning,
to get what they want out of Amway. We want Amway to
measure up to their expectations—to continue to be an opportunity that gives people hope. That's the kind of challenge Amway is to me."

The Challenges of Transition

As the founders admit, they were faced with the challenging task of balancing sibling equity with business concerns. It was not until several years after they had watched the eight children working their way up through Amway that they perceived the long-term need to pave the way for relinquishing control and turning the business over to them. They had to face the fact that they had been making too many management decisions without carrying on much dialogue with the next generation. It was indeed time to establish better communication about the vital factors of the business—such matters as finances, personnel, executive policies, and corporate goals.

The first step was the establishment of a "policy council," which found the "young eight" meeting once a month with two outside experts who trained them in group decision making. Each participant, in rotation, took his or her turn chairing the policy council to acquire experience in leadership. While the agendas of the meetings were insightful, they were not as important as the procedures required to reach a viable consensus. The goal at this stage was not to motivate the attendees to make vital policy decisions, but to bring them to the point where they could quickly and effectively resolve problems set before them.

The transition technique was a model of effectiveness. Once this educational program was in full swing, Rich and Jay started to attend the monthly meetings, at which time they would slip in detailed data about the company—its finances, its problems, its competition, its relationships with distributors, and of course its future objectives. The sessions evolved from what were basically trial run discussion groups to purposeful policy-setting roundtables. In effect, leadership was being transferred by the positive decisions of the second generation.

The significance of this course of action and the importance of the timing became evident when, in July 1992, Rich DeVos suffered a mild heart attack. Although he was hospitalized for only a short time, his condition underscored the necessity of passing the management baton down to younger leaders. Therefore, it was decided that the policy council should be dissolved and the eight sons and daughters given membership on a new Policy Board, along with Rich and Jay. They were now in an administrative position that on the one hand would give them more clout in the ongoing accomplishments of the business, but on the other hand would make them increasingly accountable for the company's problems or failures.

"Rich and I both knew," said Jay, "that someday our partnership would draw to a close, but neither of us wanted to admit that that time had come. As solid as our partnership had been in the late 1940s when we were running Wolverine Air Service or trying to sail the Caribbean, cement had been applied to that partnership through decades of hardship and triumph, affliction and prosperity. But now it was time for our partnership to make way for a new generation. We began to lay the groundwork for Rich's resignation. On Rich's recommendation and our joint decision, we settled upon Rich's eldest son, Dick, as the one who would succeed him as president."

This resolution was none too soon, for barely five months after his first heart attack, Rich suffered a second, and more serious attack. After an initial period of recovery, he bit the bullet and made his resignation. He did so knowing, of course, that the timing was appropriate, since firm plans had been made for the transition of leadership and his son had already become familiar with the role he had assumed.

By the middle of 1992, Jay Van Andel had already made

his decision to step down in a well-considered fashion from the chairmanship of the company. But the situation now left him with what he considered a very difficult choice, since he had seen through their individual performances, that all of his children were capable of corporate leadership, and he wanted to avoid favoritism at all costs. "For months I agonized over the choice," he admitted later, "praying over it and considering the issue from every possible angle."

In the end, he selected his oldest son, Steve, as the new chairman, who had long since proved himself a hard worker, with his own management style, and an excellent coalition builder. It is interesting to note, in hindsight, that in his early twenties Steve was the one who went through a period of soul-searching, was not at all sure that Amway offered the kind of career he wanted, and had a very independent mind.

Many-sided Support

Unlike a public corporation, where the board of directors plays a large part in deciding where the business is going and who will be in charge, Rich DeVos and Jay Van Andel had to carry these burdens on their own shoulders. Although decision making often put them in a somewhat lonely position, it was always reassuring that they had the full and compassionate backing and support of Amway's immense body of friends and supporters. Dick Lesher was one of these and a typical spokesperson for those friends outside the company proper. "I have known founders Rich DeVos and Jay Van Andel for more than twenty years, personally and professionally," he said. "Unlike some highly successful, wealthy people, the more you get to know Rich and Jay the more you like and respect them.

In 1996, Steve Van Andel, as chairman, and Dick DeVos, as president, published a slim folder entitled "A Foundation for Excellence," to be distributed throughout the company. They took this step, as they said in their introduction, because "it is vital for everyone in Amway to understand the philosophy upon which this business operates and the strategic direction by which it will move forward. Through awareness of these fundamental values and goals, Amway employees and distributors can partner at the highest levels and build upon our success in the coming years."

The publication pinpointed four "Founders' Fundamentals": *Freedom*, in both the personal and economic interpretations; *Family*, as our primary social structure, providing love and nurturing, heritage and legacy; *Hope*, which provides the power to transform our lives in positive ways; and *Reward*, the shared action of giving and receiving.

At the heart of the document were the following values, described as "the essential and enduring standards, not to be compromised, by which we operate the Amway business."

Partnership
Amway is built on the concept of partnership, beginning with the partnership between our founders. The partnership that exists among the founding families, distributors, and employees is our most prized possession. We always try to do what is in the long-term best interest of our partners, in a manner which increases trust and confidence. The success of Amway will reward all who have contributed to its success.

Integrity
Integrity is essential to our business success. We do what is right, not just whatever "works." Amway's success is measured not only in economic terms, but by the respect, trust, and credibility we earn.

Personal Worth
We acknowledge the uniqueness created in each individual. Every person is worthy of respect, and deserves fair treatment and the opportunity to succeed to the fullest extent of his or her potential.

Achievement
We are builders and encouragers. We strive for excellence in all we do. Our focus is on continuous improvement, progress, and achievement of individual and group goals. We anticipate change, respond swiftly to it, take action to get the job done, and gain from our experiences. We encourage creativity and innovation.

Personal Responsibility
Each individual is responsible and accountable for achieving personal goals, as well as giving 100 percent effort in helping achieve corporate or team goals. By helping people help themselves, we further the potential for individual and shared success. We also have a responsibility to be good citizens in the communities where we live and work.

Free Enterprise
We are proud advocates of freedom and free enterprise. Human economic advancement is clearly proven to be best achieved in a free market economy.

When you think of them, you immediately think of words like integrity, loyalty, devotion to family, and courage to take a stand—be it in business, politics, or life, and never mind the criticism or the consequences!

"When Rich and Jay say this business is great for families, they mean it. Amway has always been a family affair for the DeVoses and the Van Andels. All eight of their children are deeply involved in steering the company into the next century. When Rich and Jay say this business is all about helping others succeed as you succeed, they mean that too. Their friendship and partnership has lasted, solid as a rock, for more than fifty years. How many other high-profile partnerships—especially in the world of big business—can you think of that have lasted that long? From time to time, some have tried to drive a wedge between them. It never happened. It never will.''

A Legacy of Community and Accountability

"Picture Amway," said a lady who is something of an amateur poet, as well as a Direct Distributor, "not as a pond in which the beings and actions are totally contained within certain boundaries, but as a fountain that is continually splashing its waters outward, refreshing people and spots beyond the pool from which the water flows."

Her point, of course, was that Amway has a history—now a legacy, if you will—of neighborhood involvement and public service that makes its communities part of the "family." In his book *Compassionate Capitalism: People Helping People Help Themselves,* Rich DeVos listed sixteen credos for individuals and groups, and even companies, to care for people, enhance their lives, and make our planet a better place in which to live. Four of these in particular reflect the Amway philosophy of community:

- The belief that "change for the better begins when we order our lives around those individuals and institutions that we value most, for example God, country, family, friendships, schools, and work."

- The belief in "helping others to help themselves. When we share our time and money to help guide, teach, or encourage someone else, we are only giving back part of what has already been given to us."

- The belief in "helping others who cannot help themselves. When we share our time and money with those in need, we increase our own sense of dignity and self-worth, and we set in motion positive forces that bring hope and healing to the world.''

- The belief that "when we share our time, money, and experience to help others, we complete the circle of love that leads to our own personal fulfillment and prosperity.''

In this spirit of reaching out, Amway has established a multitude of scholarships, foundations, and sponsorship of museums, theaters, and projects in the arts and sciences to enhance hundreds of communities in which the company's distributors are active. A fine example of the kinds of commitments that are unusual in the business world is the Amway Environmental Foundation, which was formed to support many basic environmental education programs throughout the world. One of its purposes is to develop environmental awareness in people of all ages, to exhibit works of art that inspire respect for the ecology, and to motivate citizens to take steps to combat pollution and preserve their natural heritage. This public service program alone has earned the company dozens of awards and commendations around the globe.

The company has also helped in many ways to strengthen medical and health projects throughout the world, such as the endowment of a professorship in Disease Prevention at Stanford University's School of Medicine in California.

Not only the company in general, but Amway leaders in particular have put their pocketbook where their heart is and opened up new and vigorous opportunities that have nothing to do with their commercial operations for hundreds of thousands of people worldwide. A good "home front" example is that of the Van Andel Institute for Education and Medical Research in Grand Rapids, Michigan, one of the largest private philanthropic activities in medical research history. Founded by Jay as "a unique opportunity to pass on a legacy to all humanity that few envision and even fewer can afford," its inception received a momentous commendation from Nobel Prize–winner Michael Brown, M.D., of the University of Texas Medical Center: "We hope to create an institute that will apply the strongest aspects of basic science directly to the prevention and cure of human disease. It's very rare that an enterprise of this scope has ever begun . . . we think that the institute has the capacity in its final form to be the leading institute of medical research in the world."

Significantly, much of the decision-making and review processes are in the hands of the second generation of the family.

Amway distributors, on their own, are also catalysts in significant medical and health programs—sometimes in very remote parts of the world. One fine example is that of SAMINSA, a community relief program sponsored by Independent Amway de Mexico distributors to improve the health and decrease the poverty of the Tarahumara Indians. Another example is the public service effort of Amway Thailand, which maintains a Slum Kindergarten Improvement Program (SKIP), offering ongoing support to children through donations, outings, and other supportive and meaningful activities.

In the mid-1990s, Rich DeVos confirmed his commitment to the free enterprise system in America by establishing, as a family heritage, the Compassionate Capitalism Foundation, following the sixteen credos in his book. This nonprofit institution, he explained, has simple, basic goals: "We want to renew your faith in free enterprise, to build your hope that it is possible to cope with the change and uncertainty we are facing, and to point to compassion as our guiding light for every step of the journey.'' He announced at the time of its inception that the foundation would be giving awards each year, around the world, to individuals and institutions that are models of compassionate capitalism for the rest of us. Among the many results he hoped and expected to see in the future as a result of this philanthropic act were his beliefs that the foundation would encourage people to live up to their potential, learn to share with others, develop more positive attitudes in striving to attain goals, take steps to preserve the natural world around us, and in every sense live their lives and follow careers that recognize the values of the free enterprise system.

These are but a few examples of the legacies that Amway and its leaders have developed over the past four decades, and will continue to cultivate in the new millennium. The key word here is *accountability*. One of the company's credos expressed it this way: "If people are held accountable, they must also be free to make their own choices. Accountability and freedom go hand in hand. Accountability must always include evaluation. If people are to be held accountable, then it is necessary that their performances be evaluated and susceptible to judgment and the resulting rewards or penalties. People reap what they sow, and they must be taught in school, at home, on the job, and in all walks of life.''

CHAPTER TEN

Amway Distributor Profile

They were an attractive couple, she with her auburn hair and neatly tailored slacks and he in a business suit, as though perhaps they had just flown in for a dinner engagement. "We're Amway distributors from Richmond," she told me in a voice that had an inflection of Southern elegance.

She was a white-haired lady whom I judged to be in her early eighties. "I'm a new grandmother," she said, smiling and showing me a snapshot of an infant in arms. "But I have six other grandkids of all ages. I'm also celebrating because I just became a Ruby in my hometown, Keene, New Hampshire."

He was a strapping man, probably in his early thirties. I thought perhaps he was a professional golfer until he stuck out his hand and identified himself as an Executive Diamond from Denver.

The two young adults who greeted me shyly did not appear to be old enough to have qualified for attendance at this Amway convention. But they surprised me when they

*said they were a brother-and-sister team who had already
become Sapphires and were determined to catch up to their
parents who were Diamonds.*

*He looked like a college professor, with a beard, rum-
pled blazer, and something of a scholarly look. But not at
all. As he told me, he was a Triple Diamond and had been
a distributor "for almost a quarter of my life."*

*I had long known that Amway attracted people from just
about every walk of life. But in my discussions and interviews with several dozen people during three days at an
Amway convention, I was astonished at the diversity of jobs
and careers they had held before joining the ranks. As one
description reads, "Amway is a smorgasbord of persons.
Its rich pluralism is part of its mystique." It is certainly a
career in which there is no drawback or discrimination
because of age, sex, education, religion, color, origin, line-
age, marital status, or any other demographic classifica-
tion. Sifting through the rosters of successful distributors
you will find former doctors, nurses, engineers, soldiers,
sailors, models, entertainers, teachers, politicians, lawyers,
writers, bus drivers, secretaries, accountants, clerks—and
others who never held a steady job before in their lives.*

—*Author's recollections of an Amway convention in
Grand Rapids, Michigan*

The Big Question Mark

Probably the question most asked by people who are
being recruited as distributors is this: *How would you describe the typical person who has made a successful and
rewarding career in Amway?*

From the time we first go to school, we are taught to

believe that we should choose our future occupation or profession in terms of our abilities and training. If we are artistic, we should head in one direction, good at math in another direction, and imbued with an open nature and love of people on a completely different course. Those who are whizzes at mathematics should look for jobs in the sciences. Those who love nature and the outdoors would be most successful in fields relating to the ecology. And those who want to help their fellow beings would find life more fulfilling in fields like medicine, health, and the ministry.

But Amway is strikingly different. Defining the "typical" distributor who has made it is like trying to grasp the fabled "greased pig." A who's who of Amway over the past four decades would find examples of just about every conventional job or career description that exists—and a few that are not so conventional. One description of an Amway meeting reported that the range of people present included a former opera singer, showgirl, wrestler, professional football player, musician, dentist, airline pilot, mechanic, social director, house painter, druggist, computer programmer, mayor, preacher, commercial fisherman, detective, and even a former convict who had paid his debt to society.

Where do Amway distributors come from?

There is almost no pattern at all in this respect. They come from cities large and small, farm communities, small towns, villages, ranchlands, seaports, hill country, the plains, the woodlands, state capitals, retirement centers, hamlets, and the greatest metropolises in the world. As for places in which they function successfully and rewardingly, all of the above apply. You will find them of course in cities that are familiar to anyone, like Boston, Los Angeles, and Chicago, but also in places with names that sound like settings from a fanciful play or a romantic novel.

In like manner, you will find no peg on which to hang the description of a distributor when it comes to education, religious faith, social background, age, or heritage. And today, with the company's expansion into more than seventy lands around our planet, the diversity of backgrounds, upbringing, origins, personal history, or family status is as diverse and eclectic as the demography of the denizens of the ocean.

The fact that a person's background and training are no clues to success in Amway has been illustrated any number of times. One example, which is now a bit trite and overused but nonetheless true, are the stories of "little old ladies" who never held any conventional job, yet are successful, in contrast to hotshot salespersons with wide past experience, who come into Amway gung ho but cannot cut the mustard and have to go back to their former jobs. As might be expected, many prominent distributors *have* held challenging positions with large corporations, *have* had fine educations, and *have* been highly motivated in salaried jobs. So it would be misleading to characterize the successful distributor as a rags-to-riches person who was a low achiever for a long time before discovering what Amway had to offer them. And, while Amway has had its share of blue-collar and low-wage converts (perhaps more so in its early history or foreign operations), it has a strong reputation for attracting high percentages of executives and other top professionals with impressive career biographies.

What do others say about the Amway "prototype"?

In his book, *An Uncommon Freedom*, published when Amway was just starting its third decade, educator Charles

Paul Conn posed the question in a chapter entitled "The Amway Type." "There is a notion that those who succeed in Amway must fit some particular profile of personal traits. 'What *kind* of person can do this business?' one is asked. If a good astronaut must be cool and unflappable, an accountant must be meticulous and careful, and a good trial lawyer must be persuasive and articulate, what must a good Amway distributor be?"

His response to his own question was this: "The answer does not exist. Are good Amway distributors outgoing and extroverted? Or are they reserved and quiet? Are they well organized, detail-oriented types? Or are they spontaneous on the run planners? Do they analyze, or do they operate by instinct? Is the Amway 'type' an individual with flair and pizzazz who takes naturally to the spotlight and the speaker's stage, or is the Amway 'type' a quietly determined individual who moves steadily toward his goals with a minimum of display?

"The answer to all of these questions is *yes.*"

Conn then went on to prove his point by citing cases of distributors who fit these various classifications.

The Information Center, one of Amway's websites on the Internet, informs computer viewers that "37 percent of direct sellers have some college or technical schooling, 23 percent are college graduates, and 9 percent have done postgraduate work. Twenty-four percent are high school graduates while 7 percent did not complete high school." The report adds that "89 percent of direct sellers operate their businesses on a part-time basis, while continuing to work at a full-time job."

People build an Amway business to satisfy many different needs. Not all relate to money or material benefits. For example, people become distributors to sharpen their business skills or learn how to own and operate their own company. Others want the freedom to develop a business on their own time, at their own pace. Some want to expand their network of friends and business contacts, while others merely want the satisfaction that comes from being around so many optimistic, positive-thinking people.

Many Amway people do have one thing in common: the desire for flexibility. As the website informs us, "unlike most conventional jobs, Amway distributors can work at home, when they want, at their own pace, on their own schedule, according to the goals they have set for themselves. For some, that means that if they need an afternoon to attend a school play, see a friend, or play golf, they can arrange their work schedule to allow this. The choice of when, where, and how much time to devote to their Amway business is theirs alone. This flexibility is one important reason why the opportunity appeals to so many people around the world."

James Elliott, a longtime Amway distributor himself, expressed the opinion that Amway appealed to candidates who were people- and family-oriented. "Helping people is what attracted me to the Amway business," he said. "The business builds strong families because it gives parents an effective way to serve as good role models for their kids. . . . The most important thing Amway does is give you a chance to have a lasting impact on other people's lives. You help others reach their dreams and in turn you reach your dreams. This business works because we do it as a team."

In his book, *Rediscovering American Values,* Amway's president Dick DeVos supports this viewpoint, characterizing Direct Distributors as having one common trait at least—being very much people-oriented. As he wrote, "Amway is first and foremost a people business. Employees were often encouraged to bring their spouses to company functions.

Family members of employees were given hiring preference. Distributors were encouraged to develop their businesses as husband-and-wife teams.

"I believe that the net result of this 'family friendly' approach, which was so very innovative at the time, was the development of a high degee of loyalty and trust among Amway employees, Amway distributors, and the founding families." In his book, he further emphasizes the points that Amway was built on the idea that those who become distributors have, and are willing to take, **initiative**; that they are ready to be held **accountable** for their actions; that **perseverence** and **self-discipline** are accepted as prerequisites for success; and that **commitment** to their work and goals is essential if they are to be free and independent in their own businesses.

In regard to the subject of commitment, Dr. Helmstetter, who has spent a great deal of his professional time analyzing the personalities of distributors and what motivates them, is convinced that those who are achievers are the ones who take their business *seriously*. "I had been studying the attitudes and opportunities of Amway distributors for some time," he explained in his book, *American Victory: The Real Story of Today's Amway,* "before I decided to study the Amway *functions* themselves—and in particular who attended those functions and who stayed home." He determined that people who attended seminars and other functions were distinguished as being the most interested in getting ahead, were having more fun, were budgeting their time away as an essential part of the business, could focus more strongly on their goals, and—in summation—were serious about their involvement.

On the other side of the coin, people who did not attend functions regularly, who let other activities take priority, had little conception of the significance of the events, had little faith in themselves, were distracted by trivial pursuits, and in essence really did not take direct selling seriously.

As one of the two people most qualified of all to provide a distributor profile, Jay Van Andel had this to say in his autobiography, *An Enterprising Life*: "Some people fail to realize that Amway is not, and has never been, a get-rich-quick scheme. Some Amway distributors have become very wealthy in a short span of time. This isn't always the case, however. Most people who want to take their businesses to their greatest potential will have to do what Rich and I did when we were starting out—work long hours without quitting too easily. We realized, through our experiences with the media, that we would have to make that crystal-clear to people. The 'Amway Business Review,' which distributors hand out at all presentations of the Amway Sales and Marketing Plan, now includes information on average monthly income and bonuses for our distributors.

"Many of our meetings and rallies feature distributors who have made it big—people who are making six-figure incomes through Amway. But to look only at these success stories is to miss the really big success story—the millions of people all over the world who have a little better piece of life's goodness today because they put some of their spare time every week into Amway. In upstate New York, the mother who needs that little extra to help send her children to a parochial school and wants to work from her home. In Turkey, the father of six children who has an Amway distributorship just to buy groceries for his large family. In Japan, the businessman who sells Amway products to pay for vacations in Hawaii. Maybe they're only putting in five hours a week because their goal is just to have a little extra spending money. Maybe they're putting in ten to help send a child off to college.

"The opportunity is there, and each Amway distributor has decided for himself how far he's going to take it. We said, 'Listen, here's the deal. We've set this up so that you can make of it what you want. Don't tell us about your troubles. Don't tell us what you can't do. Just take this opportunity and show us what you can do with it.' "

The other person most qualified to characterize the nature of a successful distributor is obviously Rich DeVos. In his book, *Compassionate Capitalism,* he gives us a clear picture of the kind of person he has in mind by presenting sixteen credos that mark the individual who believes in free enterprise and, hence, in Amway's philosophy of personal achievement. The essential qualities that most come to the fore in this respect are faith in God, placing high values on family, friendship, education, and community, paying strict attention to establishing accountable financial priorities, the desire to own your own business as the best way to guarantee personal freedom, establishing goals and working diligently to achieve them, helping others to help themselves, conserving and protecting the natural world around us, and taking an honest look at where you are, where you want to be, and what you may need to change in order to get there. These are vital qualities that play a big part in determining not only who is most likely to opt for an Amway career, but who will make the most of it, both in dollars and cents and in personal growth.

What part does Amway play in "typifying" its distributors?

Although, during all of its four decades in business, the company has encouraged people to join without regard to race, religion, color, nationality, or any other demographic condition, Amway does demand certain compliances, which might in one sense pinpoint the personal characteristics of those who become distributors.

"To become an Amway distributor," explains the company's Information Center website, ''an individual must sign an agreement to abide by Amway's Rules of Conduct. Each year, they voluntarily renew that promise when they renew their Amway business.

''Our rules promote ethical direct selling principles and provide practical procedures for all distributors to observe in operating their Amway business. The Rules of Conduct mandate certain business practices. Amway has the right to enforce these rules through its contract with distributors— up to and including terminating that contract.''

Realistically, it is easy to see that some people, by nature, traits of habit, and outlooks on careers, are not likely ever to become distributors of Amway products.

In Tune with the Plan

Regardless of personality traits, goals, experience, training, and other such considerations, no one can be an Amway distributor without accepting the basic strategies and essentials of the Sales and Marketing Plan. The Amway Plan has dual goals: to create a small nucleus of repeat customers for the globally desired line of high-quality products and then duplicate the effort by enlisting others to follow suit.

Initially, all distributors had to be able to order and store the products in their homes in enough quantity to keep customers satisfied with quick delivery to fill their requests. But this procedure was modified early on in the company's history, when distributors who reached a certain level were provided with the opportunity to have orders filled directly from Amway warehouses. Today, few established distributors have to store products, and the automated supply-and-demand system is a boon to suppliers and consumers alike.

Attaining goals for greater success and profitability de-

AMWAY CODE OF ETHICS

All individuals who aspire to becoming Direct Distributors must agree to the following:

I will make the "Golden Rule" my basic principle of doing business. I will always endeavor to do unto others as I would have them do unto me.

I will uphold and follow the Rules of Conduct as stated from time to time in official Amway manuals and other literature, observing not only the letter, but also the spirit, of these Rules.

I will present Amway products and the Amway business opportunity to my customers and prospects in a truthful and honest manner, and I will make only such claims as are sanctioned in official Amway literature.

I will be courteous and prompt in handling any and all complaints, following procedures prescribed in official Amway materials for giving exchanges or refunds.

I will conduct myself in such a manner as to reflect only the highest standards of integrity, honesty, and responsibility, because I recognize that my actions as an Amway distributor have far-reaching effects, not only on my own business, but on that of other Amway distributors, as well.

I will accept and carry out the various prescribed responsibilities of an Amway distributor (and of a sponsor and a Direct Distributor when I progress to such levels of responsibility) as set forth in official Amway literature.

I will use only Amway-authorized and produced literature concerning the Amway Sales and Marketing Plan and Amway products.

pends on each distributor's ability to sponsor other distributors, who comprise their "downline." Patience is a characteristic much required in this step because a distributor can advance in profitability and standing only to the extent that the downline distributors actually sell products and keep on generating volume.

A certain orientation and degree of business sense is required to elevate a distributor from an initial standing to a level of success. There are two different criteria that are used to calculate marketing activities. The first is *Business Volume* (BV), which is a designated number for each product sold. Each product is also assigned a *Point Value* (PV), historically some 50 percent of the product's BV dollar amount. Both criteria are used to calculate the bonuses that the company or upline distributors pay, as well as to determine the tier of success a distributor has achieved under the Sales and Marketing Plan.

To become a Direct Distributor in North America, the first level of recognition, a person has to accumulate a combined PV of 7,500 a month in sales and maintain it for six months. The Plan has been somewhat modified in other countries to fit considerable differences in laws and business customs of each foreign region in which Amway operates.

The Path to Independence

For many people, this first major step, from the decision to join Amway to the initial achievement as a Direct Distributor, is often the making or breaking point. Individuals who lack motivation and a certain degree of determination just don't make it. But with the breakthrough, and a new independence on their own and away from the sponsoring distributor, Directs receive their bonuses for performance directly from Amway. At that point, too, they become eligible for additional incentives, awards, expense-paid trips, and recognition.

The most successful Amway distributors are those who then become motivated by the "giant steps" they can take—from Direct to Ruby, to Emerald, and then to several degrees of Diamond, Crown, and ultimately Crown Ambassador levels. The Diamond level, for example, is achieved when a Direct Distributor helps six different groups of distributors achieve the 7,500 Point Value.

A View from the Inside

Internally, Amway's management constantly strives—as it has done for four decades—to characterize the typical independent distributor. This is done not to go on record with statistics, but to give distributors around the world a clearer and better idea of (a) the kinds of people to try to recruit to start with, and (b) the distributors who, once brought into the fold, are the most likely to stay in the business and be successful. A good example of the kind of thinking that transpires could be seen in an *Amagram* magazine column, which was authored by Thomas W. Eggleston, former chief operating officer of Amway.

"Securing the future requires that we operate this business from a long-range perspective. It means we base our decisions and actions not just on short-term gains but on long-term prosperity. A perfect example of such is when someone builds a Crown Direct Distributorship. . . . To become a Crown requires the same traits as when you work to secure the future: commitment and fortitude. Specifically, many years of commitment for growing a business, nurturing an organization, and, simply, observing the Golden Rule. You need fortitude when tested repeatedly by personal challenges and business downturns, yet you remain focused on the future.

"One of the key concepts of sponsoring also holds true for building and sustaining a strong, long-term Amway business. Yet many distributors miss the connection and, therefore, miss potential rewards. The concept I'm referring

to is that we don't prejudge anyone—that every person has
great potential in the Amway business. In terms of sponsoring, to not prejudge is well established here: You really
cannot predict if a person will sign up as a distributor, for
people have different needs, interests, and motivations, no
matter how they come across to you.

"A surprisingly high percentage of successful Direct
Distributors are in this business for the second time. They
signed up once before, yet someone failed to follow up with
them and thus lost big bonuses from nonrenewal . . . of
those distributors who do not renew, 25 percent continue
to be customers. So they are not people who don't produce
volume. They are people who, for whatever reason, let the
renewal deadline slip past—former distributors who might
be current distributors if their uplines had devoted a little
more attention to them."

Amway Distributors Association

The ADA, composed of distributors with long experience in their careers, works together with the Amway Corporation to provide distributors with the best possible
business environment in the matter of mutual business relationships. The ADA keeps distributors up to date on new
business issues, the creation and inauguration of new products, reviews of and any amendments to the distributors'
Rules of Conduct, and changing developments in Amway's
increasing and spreading global operations. The ADA
maintains a thirty-member board that also serves as a
sounding board for distributors who have complaints of any
nature, need advice about problems they cannot resolve in-
dependently, or have innovative suggestions about ways to
improve business.

One example of subject areas that have concerned the

board in recent years has to do with the Americans with Disabilities Act of 1990. Shortly after the passing of the Act, the board strongly advised distributors that they should be familiar with this legislation, particularly in their recruitment programs and dealing with customers. As it was explained, the law prohibits discrimination on the basis of disability in the enjoyment of goods, services, facilities, privileges, advantages, or accommodations of any place of public accommodation. The law requires that all public accommodations provide auxiliary aids or services to ensure that individuals with disabilities are not excluded, denied services, segregated, or otherwise treated differently from other individuals, unless it can be demonstrated that the provision of these aids or services would constitute an undue burden. Here for example, are some answers to common questions about the law that have been asked by Amway distributors and answered by the board:

What is a "public accommodation"?

A place generally open to the public. If you hold a function in a public accommodation, such as a hotel or convention center, your function becomes a public accommodation, regardless of whether it is open to the public.

Can a distributor's private residence be a public accommodation?

No. Your private residence, or the private residences of your downlines, prospects, or customers, does not become a public accommodation as a result of housing a distributor function, as these places are not open to the public.

Who is responsible for compliance—the facility or the distributor who rents space?

If you hold a function in a public accommodation, you share equal responsibility for compliance with all provisions of the Act with the event facility. Many facilities now have a provision in their contracts that allocates the responsibilities, making the facility responsible for the removal of barriers (such as installing ramps and making rest rooms wheelchair-accessible) and making you responsible for providing nondiscriminatory services (such as sign-language interpreters for hearing-impaired individuals).

What are the penalties for noncompliance?

The court in a civil action brought by either an individual or the attorney general may grant any equitable relief it considers appropriate, including fines up to $50,000 for a first violation and up to $100,000 for subsequent violations. For more data, a two-page handout is available from Amway's Distributor Relations Division. We want to make sure that everyone has an equal opportunity with the Amway opportunity.

A great majority of the people who elect to become distributors have done so, now as in the past, because they want to be *independent*. But, as Amway has been the first to point out, independence in itself demands certain responsibilities—including many that are not required of individuals who work in salaried positions in the business world. Thus, some people, who at first may seem to have the individual characteristics and personalities to be independent, have found that they were not prepared to take on the responsibilities demanded.

Personal Discipline

"An important choice you have to make regards discipline," Rich DeVos often used to say to distributors. "You can be easy on yourself or you can be tough on yourself. If you choose to be lax, everything you do is likely to fit the same pattern. If you exert proper discipline, your body and mental attitudes will reflect that, and you are much more likely to get jobs done, avoid procrastination, and really get to enjoy what you are doing. It is much like going out for a sport. You end up getting out of it exactly what you put into it. If you will condition your body to the exacting requirements of the sport (or job), you will be rewarded with many more satisfactions than if you elect to follow the lazy route, sit back, and let others take over."

Distributors are advised to evaluate their time and analyze how much they devote to "accentuating the positive." Discipline, they are told, becomes very important as individuals mature because it develops good habits and contributes to their ability to learn. Appearance is important too, and discipline can help to keep people slim, in good health, and vigorous. Once they forfeit discipline, they are more likely to slip into sloppy ways in all departments.

"One problem we all face regularly is to get down to the things we have to do," emphasized DeVos. "The first step in overcoming this very human weakness is to recognize the fact that discipline is not easy. No matter who you are or where you are or how smart you are, discipline is against human nature. So you are already fighting the system, as it were. The second step is to understand that a good many disciplines are established early in life. Going to church, for example, is a discipline that some people have and others do not. Changes in discipline are likely to occur when there are crises—a panic, an epidemic, a scare brought on by a serious threat to one's health, or perhaps poverty or hunger or family emotional upheavals.

"What are some of the events that cause people to sit back and reconsider their lives and their activities? They might include a death in the family, the case of a son or daughter who leaves home abruptly under bitter circumstances, or a health episode that makes one think more seriously about weight, diet, and lifestyle. Some psychologists call these *trigger points*. They are the events or circumstances that make people change their viewpoints and habits, that make them finally come round to disciplining themselves in order to counteract the problems or threats."

For distributors having trouble with discipline, the following are ploys they can use to prompt themselves into taking proper action. Among these are:

- Blocking out a period of time each day in which to complete a set chore.

- Working with other people so that a group, and not just an individual, is involved in something that has to be done, or should be done, regularly.

- Keeping a score card on activities like exercise or diet or task performance.

- Giving yourself some kind of reward each time you complete a certain routine.

- Taping a picture in a prominent place (such as the refrigerator) to depict something that you will be rewarded with if you discipline yourself properly.

- Making a boring routine more exciting through the use of some kind of gimmick.

"People are often too impatient to impose proper discipline on themselves," DeVos added. "They ignore the fact that it often takes a long time to establish a solid pattern, sometimes years, whereas a lot of people think they are going to do that in a week or a month. You see this all the time with people who go on diets. They diet for sixty days and lose weight and then within thirty more days they have put it all back on. Why? Because they never really did establish the pattern so that it would work."

The founders of Amway found early on in molding the company that one of the most effective forms of self-discipline was working with other people, a principle that has been followed by their sons and daughters now managing Amway. When working in a group, you can accomplish some things more easily and continually than when trying to do it by yourself.

Doing things with other people is one positive form of motivation, it is pointed out. You don't have to go to college at all, for example, to acquire knowledge that can be learned through printed books and videotapes and audiotapes. But when you go to college you become part of a group and the studying becomes more palatable than doing it all by yourself, as a loner. With the kinds of visual aids we have today for home study, not to mention the remarkable strides in computer programming, there is no reason why an entire education cannot be acquired at home. But few people have the discipline to do this effectively.

Taking the Most Satisfying Choice

It was mentioned earlier that reducing boredom is an antidote to some chore that is necessary but boring. A good example is the stationary bicycle, which was invented as a handy way of getting exercise similar to bicycling down the street, but without having to leave the house, dress properly, or face inclement weather. The problem was that this kind of pedaling was nowhere near as interesting as riding along a highway or path where there was something to see. So people used the device of watching TV, reading books, or listening to music and audio programs on tape as they worked off the calories in the privacy of their homes.

When you are in business for yourself, as an entrepreneur, cautions Amway, you need different disciplines to keep motivated. It becomes very important to become disciplined because you don't have people telling you when to do things or setting deadlines. You are your own taskmaster. When you are working in a structured business, you just have to do what you are supposed to do or eventually you will be fired. Also, you have to go to a certain place regularly and follow certain patterns of work and responsibility. The discipline is set for you. Without having developed the pattern of doing things when you have your own business, you will fail. You have to evolve a routine. It always helps to have two or more people working together because teamwork is an effective form of discipline.

If you can provide reinforcement for your goals and get family members involved, you may proceed faster. You should also have a way of rewarding yourself when you do attain a goal, or step toward a goal. If you lose a certain number of pounds, say, or reach a stage in some other form of self-improvement, acknowledge it. It helps here, of course, to have children or other family members who share in the rewards or at least can cheer you on.

That is what Amway is all about—and has been throughout its history.

The Three A's: *Attitude, Action, Atmosphere*

In the 1960s, during a period when the country was in an upheaval about such matters as the Cuban missile crisis, the Kennedy assassination, the war in Vietnam, drug addiction by American students, and violent civil rights clashes, Rich DeVos asserted that, despite the disturbances on many fronts, "these are great days in which we live—the best of times, even though some people groan that it is the worst of times."

How could this be? As he said then, "Despite the fears of the naysayers, the country in general and most communities as a part of the whole are in fine shape. Most people enjoy decent jobs; spendable income is up; inflation has been held in check; and there are more opportunities—economically, socially, recreationally, culturally, and spiritually—than in any other nation in the world.

"As we like to say in our own business, 'Let us run while others walk.' "

One successful Amway program, from the standpoint of distributor communication and personal guidance, was referred to as "The Three A's." It was described in the following manner:

In every major venture there is a tripartite pattern that we refer to us "The Three A's," which influences the turn of events and the people who participate in those events:

Action is the goal on which we set our sights, whether we are selling products, trying to influence people to reach certain decisions, planning the construction of a large building, supporting the arts, running for public office, or becoming involved in almost any other field of human endeavor.

Attitude fits quickly into place because much of the suc-

*cess of achieving action depends upon our attitudes. Even
when raising young children, you can demand an action,
but the demand grows weaker and weaker as they grow
older unless positive attitudes have been molded. What we
do in effect is to try to reinforce an attitude that achieves
the ends we cannot force by taking action. We may not be
able to force action, so we turn to attitude. We have a little
better chance of motivating someone to do something if we
can mold an attitude or attitudes. No matter how constructive or great we think our attitudes are, we can hope for
no more than to convince other people that we are right.
But we cannot force them to think that way. Giving a sense
of confidence is one means of helping to shape attitudes.
But one person cannot tell other persons that their attitudes
must be such and such.*

*Atmosphere is the third leg of the triangle and the only
one of the three that we can control. Once you understand
this, you will stop trying to force action or change attitudes.
Atmosphere is what provides the motivation for attitudes
and actions. When we are fully aware of the power of atmosphere, then we can use it to influence the first two elements, Action and Attitude. We grow up in different
communities—"atmospheres" if you will—some of us in
favorable ones, which were basically beneficial, others in
unpleasant atmospheres, which tended to foster disharmo-
nies and regrets. No matter what endeavor you undertake,
if you get people to breathe the right air, then that atmosphere becomes a strong, positive force in moving people
and motivating them.*

CHAPTER ELEVEN

The Millennium

As Amway looks to the next millennium, it will continue to strive to bring the Amway opportunity and the spirit of free enterprise to people everywhere. With continued growth, the Amway of the future undoubtedly will look very different from the Amway of today on the surface. But underneath, the unimpeachable values and ethics on which Jay and Rich built their business and their lives, the concept that Amway must do what is right, not just what works, will remain unchanged. The commitment to helping others instilled in Rich and Jay by their parents is a legacy that has been handed down to their children, who are dedicated to carrying on the long tradition of partnership between business and the community.

It is this spirit of partnership, between the Van Andel and DeVos families, between Amway Corporation and Amway distributors, and between Amway and the community, that will lead Amway to realizing its vision: ***"To be the best business opportunity in the world."***

—"Summation for the Future" on Amway's website

Tomorrow and Tomorrow

Although prognostications for the future are often as elusive as next year's weather prediction, and customarily dependent upon the powers of imagination of the forecaster, Amway does not have the luxury of making snap judgments. The company's management knows, for example, that it is likely to lose the confidence of many thousands of distributors in the field if it constantly makes rosy, but wishful, predictions in the home office. For the beginning of the next century, Amway bases its forecasts on the following kinds of operations and relationships, among others:

Reinvestment: Aggressive reinvestment of capital in the business with the specific objective of introducing new plans and reinforcing old ones to help distributors increase their long-term sales and upgrade their sponsoring activities.

Product Innovation and Improvement: Painstaking research and development to add new products where appropriate and improve the capabilities and competence of existing ones in the lineup to retain a constant competitive edge in the marketplace.

Strategic Alliances: Collaboration with other companies whose brand-name products are widely recognized for their quality and performance. Recent examples have been the alliances with Rubbermaid and Waterford.

Backup Programs: Reaching out around the globe has seen, and will continue to see, an ever-expanding support network to help all distributors, maximize communications and consignment, and minimize transportation delays. Examples of this kind of activity are seen in special manufacturing facilities when called for and the proliferation of Regional Distribution Centers that greatly expand product distribution capacity.

Targeted Marketing: Intensive studies of markets with the objective of providing distributors with enhanced orientation and facilities to grow under existing market conditions in their specific marketing areas.

Expanded and Improved Visibility: Increasing public awareness of Amway products through advertising, promotion, public relations, and public service in fields like education, health, conservation, seminars, and sports, and the sponsorship of regional, national, and international events.

Greater Rewards and Recognition: The creation and development of a three-year program of increased incentives, which started in 1998, to encourage distributors to build their businesses and manage their teams for long-term growth.

Millennium Growth Awards: Offering higher-level distributors a means of qualifying for annual bonuses and a "growth sharing" bonus in the year 2000.

To make certain that growth blueprints for the future meet distributor approval—whether for improvements in the Sales and Marketing Plan, advertising, websites, business policies, new affiliates, expansions of the customer base, or other areas of operation and commitment—the issues and options are constantly reviewed, discussed, and accepted or rejected by the Amway Distributors Association board and its executive committee. Business ethics, legal affairs, international procedures, and awards and recognition are also vital review areas. One of the association's major commitments is to maintain its agenda for growth—a plan of action for increasing the size of the Amway business from now until well into the twenty-first century—while at the same time assuring the historical excellence and depth of service. It has not been unusual for monthly meetings to require four days of discussion and decision making, and to last from nine in the morning until well past midnight.

There are two target areas relating to the future: the broad overall Millennium Growth study and individual geographic studies, such as the Amway North America (ANA) Growth Program. One example of the former is an agenda to provide direction on how the company can best inform its distributors about the legal, technical, financial, and ethical complexities of doing business in foreign markets. This includes a presentation, entitled ''Pre-Launch Rules,'' which emphasizes strict procedures and provides guidelines for establishing an international affiliate before actually starting the business.

Goals: Key to the Future

''It is essential,'' warned Jay Van Andel, as he neared the time he had selected for retirement, ''that we not focus simply on past successes. After a while, if we don't continue to innovate, the competition will move up on us, reducing the edge we hold over them, and their products will become a lot like our products. We have to keep open the cutting edge of technology and product development.''

At the beginning of the 1990s, Rich DeVos asked this question, with his mind on the company's future for the next decade: *Why are goals so important to our success, and how do we make and keep them?* Answering his own question, and looking forward to the next decade, he said, ''We believe that success comes only to those who establish goals and then work diligently to achieve them. . . . We should begin immediately to determine our short-term and long-term goals, to write them down, to review our progress at every step, to celebrate the goals we accomplish, and to learn from those we don't.''

Speaking of his own accomplishments, he reminded readers that it had taken him "half a lifetime" to see his own goal come true, that he had his own share of detours, and "even a disaster or two," before finding success, and that people in Amway should take a long, hard look at the future and not expect prosperity to come overnight. Long-range goals are really about creating and attaining a series of short-range goals. "Plans outline where you want to go," he wrote. "They give you ways to measure progress. They give you a sense of clear direction and of purpose. Remember the bumper sticker: *Stand for something or you'll fall for anything.*"

Today Rich's son Dick, now the president of Amway, echoed his father's vision, despite the fact that the world seems to be facing increasing problems and threats to freedom. "Although I continue to be optimistic about the future of our great land and our virtually unlimited potential to lead the peoples of the world in the right direction," he wrote, "I do believe that we are facing a crisis of character that threatens the fundamental integrity of our nation. If we want the next generation of Americans to have the freedom our forefathers intended, then we must teach them, by example, to 'do what is right.' We must provide our children, the youth who will serve as our leaders in the new millennium, with the proper foundation. We must teach them the importance of the values that make freedom possible.

"For this reason, I challenge all who read this to rediscover our American values. Be bold. Take the first step today. Smile at someone. Be humble in your achievements. Work hard. Send a note of appreciation to a friend or colleague. Volunteer to help in your community. Tutor a child. Be someone's big brother or big sister. The list of opportunities is endless.

"The important thing is that you make the effort and

follow through on your commitment. I am an eternal optimist, I know we can put the shine back on the *golden door*. And the luster it provides will once again be the beacon for all who seek freedom. It is a dream and conviction of mine to preserve the dreams of those who came before us . . . to protect freedom in this 'promised land.' It is my hope and prayer that . . . this will become your dream and conviction as well.''

"We dare not just look back to great yesterdays. We must look forward to great tomorrows."

—*Adlai E. Stevenson*

APPENDIX

Amway Awards and Rewards

Distributor
Earn profits through retail mark-up on products sold, plus bonuses of 3 to 25 percent based on Point Value (PV), which averages approximately 50 percent of wholesale price paid on total business volume.

Silver Producer
For one month, generate personal group PV of at least 7,500 points, or sponsoring a 25 percent group (one containing a qualifying Silver Producer or Direct Distributor) and generating at a personal group PV of at least 2,500 points, or sponsor two 25 percent groups in the same month, or foster sponsor a 25 percent group and have PV or 2,500 points.

Gold Producer
Generate three Silver Producer months in a year.

Direct Distributor
For 6 months of a fiscal year, generate PV of at least 7,500 personal group points or sponsor a 25 percent group with

2,500 personal group points or sponsor two 25 percent groups in those months or foster sponsor a 25 percent group plus achieve PV of at least 2,500 points.

Founders Direct Distributor Pin
Maintain twelve months of Direct Distributor qualification in a fiscal year.

Ruby Direct Distributor
Generate personal group PV of 15,000 or more points in a given month.

Founders Ruby Pin
Maintain Ruby qualification for twelve months within a fiscal year.

Sapphire Pin
Direct Distributors below Emerald who have either 3 North American groups qualifying for 6 months in a fiscal year; or 2,500 Award Volume over the same two qualified North American groups for each of 6 months in the fiscal year; or a combination of both.

Emerald Direct Distributor
Direct Distributors who personally, internationally, or foster sponsor three or more qualified groups for at least six months of a fiscal year.

Founders Emerald Pin
Maintain Emerald qualifications for twelve months within a fiscal year.

Diamond Direct Distributor
Direct Distributors who personally, internationally, or foster sponsor six qualified groups (at least three in North America) for at least six months of the fiscal year.

Additional Pin Levels

Executive Diamond personally, internationally, or foster sponsor nine qualified groups (at least three in North America) for at least six months of the fiscal year; a Double Diamond does so with twelve groups, a Triple Diamond with fifteen groups, a Crown Direct with eighteen groups, and a Crown Ambassador with twenty groups.

Glossary

BENEFITS. All types of compensation, including markups, commissions, bonuses, overrides, and personal advantages such as insurance, travel, and the use of a vehicle.

BUSINESS VOLUME. Also referred to as BV, this is a method used to calculate commissions and overrides instead of using dollar amounts. (See Point Volume).

BUYBACK. Company agreement to accept the return of unsold products for a full or partial refund.

COMMISSION. A fee paid on the sale of a product or service.

CONSULTANT. An independent marketing expert used by some companies to assist and advise distributors.

DIRECT DISTRIBUTOR. The first level, reached after making a predetermined amount of sales.

DIRECT SALES. A method of selling in which manufacturers or marketers reach consumers with their products through a personal sales contact. All multilevel businesses employ direct selling, but not all direct sales firms use multilevel marketing.

DISTRIBUTOR. An agent who works through an agreement with a manufacturer and is eligible to represent the company in the marketing of its products as an independent businessperson.

DOWNLINE. The line of sponsorship between a distributor and all sponsorship levels below.

FRONT LOADING. A practice, often deemed unethical, whereby new distributors are pressured into buying an unnecessarily large supply of products at the start, or otherwise making financial commitments that are excessive.

LEG. A new distributor personally sponsored by an existing distributor, as well as others down the line.

LEVEL. The position a distributor holds in the organization, as distinguished by such terms as *Pearl, Emerald,* and *Diamond.*

MULTILEVEL MARKETING. Also referred to as MLM, this is a method of selling in which customers have the option of becoming distributors, who in turn develop downlines, and in which all share in the profits in proportion to their levels.

NETWORK MARKETING. A synonym for multilevel marketing.

OPPORTUNITY MEETING. Any meeting in which distributors present sales and business opportunities to likely prospects who might then become their downlines.

OVERRIDES. Money paid on downline production.

PIN AWARDS. Pins used to recognize a distributor's rise to a new status level, commonly using gemstones, such as pearl, emerald, or ruby in their design.

POINT VOLUME. Known as PV, this is an index used to calculate commissions and overrides instead of using dollar amounts.

PYRAMID SCHEME. An illegal business that superficially resembles legitimate direct selling or multilevel marketing, but which generates income solely by recruiting new members and charging them fees. This is similar in effect to a chain letter that requests a payment from recipients with the promise that they will get their money back, many times multiplied, by sending similar letters to others.

RENEWAL. A periodic (usually annual) agreement to continue in practice as a distributor, or other independent representative of a company.

RESIDUAL INCOME. Profits that continue to arrive after the activities generating the income have ended.

SALES VOLUME. Calculated in terms of personal sales volume (PSV), the amount of goods and services you personally have sold or group sales volume (GSV), the amount sold, by you and your downlines.

SPONSOR. The person who has recruited a distributor and bears the responsibility for indoctrinating, training, and advising that person.

UPLINE. The line of sponsorship between a particular distributor and the sponsoring levels above. A sponsor is, therefore, an upline.

The Amway Secret of Success:
How to Turn Indecision into Inspiration

This is the book that was based on interviews
with the founders of Amway, two of the world's
most prosperous businessmen, who revealed to
the author many of their tips for personal
success and achievement.

Choices with Clout

How to Make Things Happen by Making the
Right Decisions Every Day of Your Life

by Wilbur Cross

• NOW PUBLISHED IN EIGHT FOREIGN EDITIONS

❏ 0-425-14538-7/$5.99

Prices slightly higher in Canada

Payable in U.S. funds only. No cash/COD accepted. Postage & handling: U.S./CAN. $2.75 for one book, $1.00 for each additional, not to exceed $6.75; Int'l $5.00 for one book, $1.00 each additional. We accept Visa, Amex, MC ($10.00 min.), checks ($15.00 fee for returned checks) and money orders.   Call 800-788-6262 or 201-933-9292, fax 201-896-8569; refer to ad # 840 (6/99)

Penguin Putnam Inc.   Bill my: ❏ Visa ❏ MasterCard ❏ Amex _____(expires)
P.O. Box 12289, Dept. B
Newark, NJ 07101-0289   Card#
Please allow 4-6 weeks for delivery.   Signature _____
Foreign and Canadian delivery 6-8 weeks.

Bill to:
Name _____
Address _____City _____
State/ZIP _____Daytime Phone # _____
Ship to:
Name _____Book Total $ _____
Address _____Applicable Sales Tax $ _____
City _____Postage & Handling $ _____
State/ZIP _____Total Amount Due $ _____
This offer subject to change without notice.